Teachings of Jesus of Nazareth

1 Thirty Years of Preparation

1.1 *The Beginning*
The Good News about Jesus Christ, the Son of God, begins with what the prophet Isaiah said would happen.[1]

Most Honorable Theophilus: Many others have tried to give a report of the things that happened among us to complete God's plan. What they have written agrees with what we learned from the people who saw those events from the beginning. They also served God by telling people his message. I studied it all carefully from the beginning. Then I decided to write it down for you in an organized way. I did this so that you can be sure that what you have been taught is true.[2]

Before the world began, the Word was there. The Word was with God, and the Word was God. He was there with God in the beginning. Everything was made through him, and nothing was made without him. In him there was life, and that life was a light for the people of the world. The light shines in the darkness, and the darkness has not defeated it.

There was a man named John, who was sent by God. He came to tell people about the light. Through him all people could hear about the light and believe. John was not the light. But he came to tell people about the light. The true light was coming into the world. This is the true light that gives light to all people.

The Word was already in the world. The world was made through him, but the world did not know him. He came to the world that was his own. And his own people did not accept him. But some people did accept him. They believed in him, and he gave them the right to become children of God. They became God's children, but not in the way babies are usually born. It was not because of any human desire or plan. They were born from God himself.

The Word became a man and lived among us. We saw his divine greatness—the greatness that belongs to the only Son of the Father.

The Word was full of grace and truth. John told people about him. He said loudly, "This is the one I was talking about when I said, 'The one who is coming after me is greater than I am, because he was living before I was even born.'"

Yes, the Word was full of grace and truth, and from him we all received one blessing after another. That is, the law was given to us through Moses, but grace and truth came through Jesus Christ. No one has ever seen God. The only Son is the one who has shown us what God is like. He is himself God and is very close to the Father.[3]

1.2 The Birth of John the Baptizer Foretold

During the time when Herod ruled Judea, there was a priest named Zechariah. He belonged to Abijah's group. His wife came from the family of Aaron. Her name was Elizabeth. Zechariah and Elizabeth were both good people who pleased God. They did everything the Lord commanded, always following his instructions completely. But they had no children. Elizabeth could not have a baby, and both of them were very old.

Zechariah was serving as a priest before God for his group. It was his group's time to serve. The priests always chose one priest to offer the incense, and Zechariah was the one chosen this time. So he went into the Temple of the Lord to offer the incense. There was a large crowd outside praying at the time the incense was offered.

Then, on the right side of the incense table an angel of the Lord came and stood before Zechariah. When he saw the angel, Zechariah was upset and very afraid. But the angel said to him, "Zechariah, don't be afraid. Your prayer has been heard by God. Your wife Elizabeth will give birth to a baby boy, and you will name him John. You will be very happy, and many others will share your joy over his birth. He will be a great man for the Lord. He will never drink wine or liquor. Even before he is born, he will be filled with the Holy Spirit.

"John will help many people of Israel return to the Lord their God. John himself will go ahead of the Lord and make people ready for his coming. He will be powerful like Elijah and will have the same spirit. He will make peace between fathers and their children. He will cause people who are not obeying God to change and start thinking the way they should."

Zechariah said to the angel, "How can I know that what you say is true? I am an old man, and my wife is also old."

The angel answered him, "I am Gabriel, the one who always stands ready before God. He sent me to talk to you and to tell you this good news. Now, listen! You will not be able to talk until the day when these things happen. You will lose your speech because you did not believe what I told you. But everything I said will really happen."

Outside, the people were still waiting for Zechariah. They were surprised that he was staying so long in the Temple. Then Zechariah came outside, but he could not speak to them. So the people knew that he had seen a vision inside the Temple. He was not able to speak, so he could only make signs to the people. When his time of service was finished, he went home.

Later, Zechariah's wife Elizabeth became pregnant. So she did not go out of her house for five months. She said, "Look what the Lord has done for me! He decided to help me. Now people will stop thinking there is something wrong with me."[4]

1.3 *The Birth of Jesus Foretold*

During Elizabeth's sixth month of pregnancy, God sent the angel Gabriel to a virgin girl who lived in Nazareth, a town in Galilee. She was engaged to marry a man named Joseph from the family of David. Her name was Mary. The angel came to her and said, "Greetings! The Lord is with you; you are very special to him."

But Mary was very confused about what the angel said. She wondered, "What does this mean?"

The angel said to her, "Don't be afraid, Mary, because God is very pleased with you. Listen! You will become pregnant and have a baby boy. You will name him Jesus. He will be great. People will call him the Son of the Most High God, and the Lord God will make him king like his ancestor David. He will rule over the people of Jacob forever; his kingdom will never end."

Mary said to the angel, "How will this happen? I am still a virgin."

The angel said to Mary, "The Holy Spirit will come to you, and the power of the Most High God will cover you. The baby will be holy and will be called the Son of God. And here's something else: Your relative Elizabeth is pregnant. She is very old, but she is going to have a son. Everyone thought she could not have a baby, but she has been pregnant now for six months. God can do anything!"

Mary said, "I am the servant of the Lord God. Let this thing you have said happen to me!" Then the angel went away.[5]

1.4 Mary Visits Elizabeth

Mary got up and went quickly to a town in the hill country of Judea. She went into Zechariah's house and greeted Elizabeth. When Elizabeth heard Mary's greeting, the unborn baby inside her jumped, and she was filled with the Holy Spirit.

In a loud voice she said to Mary, "God has blessed you more than any other woman. And God has blessed the baby you will have. You are the mother of my Lord, and you have come to me! Why has something so good happened to me? When I heard your voice, the baby inside me jumped with joy. Great blessings are yours because you believed what the Lord said to you! You believed this would happen."[6]

1.5 Mary Praises God

Then Mary said,

"I praise the Lord with all my heart.
   I am very happy because God is my Savior.
I am not important,
   but he has shown his care for me, his lowly servant.
From now until the end of time,
   people will remember how much God blessed me.
Yes, the Powerful One has done great things for me.
   His name is very holy.
He always gives mercy to those who worship him.
He reached out his arm and showed his power.
   He scattered those who are proud and think great things about themselves.
He brought down rulers from their thrones
   and raised up the humble people.
He filled the hungry with good things,
   but he sent the rich away with nothing.
God has helped Israel—the people he chose to serve him.
   He did not forget his promise to give us his mercy.
He has done what he promised to our ancestors, to Abraham and his children forever."

Mary stayed with Elizabeth for about three months and then went home.[7]

1.6 The Birth of John the Baptizer

When it was time for Elizabeth to give birth, she had a boy. Her neighbors and relatives heard that the Lord was very good to her, and they were happy for her.

When the baby was eight days old, they came to circumcise him. They wanted to name him Zechariah because this was his father's name. But his mother said, "No, he will be named John."

The people said to Elizabeth, "But no one in your family has that name." Then they made signs to his father, "What would you like to name him?"

Zechariah asked for something to write on. Then he wrote, "His name is John." Everyone was surprised. Then Zechariah could talk again, and he began praising God. And all their neighbors were afraid. In all the hill country of Judea people continued talking about these things. Everyone who heard about these things wondered about them. They thought, "What will this child be?" They could see that the Lord was with him.[8]

1.7 Zechariah Praises God

Then Zechariah, John's father, was filled with the Holy Spirit and told the people a message from God:

"Praise to the Lord God of Israel.
    He has come to help his people and has given them freedom.
He has given us a powerful Savior
    from the family of his servant David.
This is what he promised
    through his holy prophets long ago.
He will save us from our enemies
    and from the power of all those who hate us.
God said he would show mercy to our fathers,
    and he remembered his holy agreement.
This was the promise he made to our father Abraham,
    a promise to free us from the power of our enemies,
    so that we could serve him without fear
    in a way that is holy and right for as long as we live.

"Now you, little boy, will be called a prophet of the Most High God.
   You will go first before the Lord to prepare the way for him.
   You will make his people understand that they will be saved by
      having their sins forgiven.

"With the loving mercy of our God,
   a new day from heaven will shine on us.
   It will bring light to those who live in darkness, in the fear of
      death.
   It will guide us into the way that brings peace."

And so the little boy John grew up and became stronger in spirit. Then he lived in areas away from other people until the time when he came out to tell God's message to the people of Israel.[9]

1.8 *The Birth of Jesus*

This is how the birth of Jesus Christ happened. His mother Mary was engaged to marry Joseph. But before they married, he learned that she was expecting a baby. (She was pregnant by the power of the Holy Spirit.) Mary's husband, Joseph, was a good man. He did not want to cause her public disgrace, so he planned to divorce her secretly.

But after Joseph thought about this, an angel from the Lord came to him in a dream. The angel said, "Joseph, son of David, don't be afraid to accept Mary to be your wife. The baby inside her is from the Holy Spirit. She will give birth to a son. You will name him Jesus. Give him that name because he will save his people from their sins."

All this happened to make clear the full meaning of what the Lord said through the prophet: "The virgin will be pregnant and will give birth to a son. They will name him Immanuel." (Immanuel means "God with us.")

When Joseph woke up, he did what the Lord's angel told him to do. He married Mary. But Joseph did not have sexual relations with her until her son was born.[10]

It was about that same time that Augustus Caesar sent out an order to all people in the countries that were under Roman rule. The order said that everyone's name must be put on a list. This was the first counting of all the people while Quirinius was governor of Syria. Everyone traveled to their own hometowns to have their name put on the list.

So Joseph left Nazareth, a town in Galilee, and went to the town of Bethlehem in Judea. It was known as the town of David. Joseph went there because he was from the family of David. Joseph registered with Mary because she was engaged to marry him. (She was now pregnant.) While Joseph and Mary were in Bethlehem, the time came for her to have the baby. She gave birth to her first son. She wrapped him up well and laid him in a box where cattle are fed. She put him there because the guest room was full.[11]

1.9 Shepherds Hear About Jesus

That night, some shepherds were out in the fields near Bethlehem watching their sheep. An angel of the Lord appeared to them, and the glory of the Lord was shining around them. The shepherds were very afraid. The angel said to them, "Don't be afraid. I have some very good news for you—news that will make everyone happy. Today your Savior was born in David's town. He is Christ, the Lord. This is how you will know him: You will find a baby wrapped in pieces of cloth and lying in a feeding box."

Then a huge army of angels from heaven joined the first angel, and they were all praising God, saying,

"Praise God in heaven,
 and on earth let there be peace to the people who please him."

The angels left the shepherds and went back to heaven. The shepherds said to each other, "What a great event this is that the Lord has told us about. Let's go to Bethlehem and see it."

So they went running and found Mary and Joseph. And there was the baby, lying in the feeding box. When they saw the baby, they told what the angels said about this child. Everyone was surprised when they heard what the shepherds told them. Mary continued to think about these things, trying to understand them. The shepherds went back to their sheep, praising God and thanking him for everything they had seen and heard. It was just as the angel had told them.

When the baby was eight days old, he was circumcised, and he was named Jesus. This name was given by the angel before the baby began to grow inside Mary.[12]

1.10 Jesus Is Presented in the Temple

The time came for Mary and Joseph to do the things the Law of Moses taught about being made pure. They brought Jesus to Jerusalem so that they could present him to the Lord. It is written in the law of the Lord: "When a mother's first baby is a boy, he shall be called 'special for the Lord.'" The law of the Lord also says that people must give a sacrifice: "You must sacrifice two doves or two young pigeons." So Joseph and Mary went to Jerusalem to do this.

A man named Simeon lived in Jerusalem. He was a good man who was devoted to God. He was waiting for the time when God would come to help Israel. The Holy Spirit was with him. The Holy Spirit told him that he would not die before he saw the Christ from the Lord. The Spirit led Simeon to the Temple. So he was there when Mary and Joseph brought the baby Jesus to do what the Jewish law said they must do. Simeon took the baby in his arms and thanked God:

"Now, Lord, you can let me, your servant, die in peace as you said.
I have seen with my own eyes how you will save your people.
Now all people can see your plan.
He is a light to show your way to the other nations.
And he will bring honor to your people Israel."

Jesus' father and mother were amazed at what Simeon said about him. Then Simeon blessed them and said to Mary, "Many Jews will fall and many will rise because of this boy. He will be a sign from God that some will not accept. So the secret thoughts of many will be made known. And the things that happen will be painful for you—like a sword cutting through your heart."

Anna, a prophetess, was there at the Temple. She was from the family of Phanuel in the tribe of Asher. She was now very old. She had lived with her husband seven years before he died and left her alone. She was now 84 years old. Anna was always at the Temple; she never left. She worshiped God by fasting and praying day and night.

Anna was there when Joseph and Mary came to the Temple. She praised God and talked about Jesus to all those who were waiting for God to free Jerusalem.[13]

1.11 Wise Men Come to Visit Jesus

Jesus was born in the town of Bethlehem in Judea during the time when Herod was king. After Jesus was born, some wise men from the east came to Jerusalem. They asked people, "Where is the child who has been born to be the king of the Jews? We saw the star that shows he was born. We saw it rise in the sky in the east and have come to worship him."

When King Herod heard about this, it upset him as well as everyone else in Jerusalem. Herod called a meeting of all the leading Jewish priests and teachers of the law. He asked them where the Messiah would be born. They answered, "In the town of Bethlehem in Judea, just as the prophet wrote:

'Bethlehem, in the land of Judah,
   you are important among the rulers of Judah.
Yes, a ruler will come from you,
   and that ruler will lead Israel, my people.'"

Then Herod had a private meeting with the wise men from the east. He learned from them the exact time they first saw the star. Then he sent them to Bethlehem. He said, "Go and look carefully for the child. When you find him, come tell me. Then I can go worship him too."

After the wise men heard the king, they left. They saw the same star they had seen in the east, and they followed it. The star went before them until it stopped above the place where the child was. They were very happy and excited to see the star.

The wise men came to the house where the child was with his mother Mary. They bowed down and worshiped him. Then they opened the boxes of gifts they had brought for him. They gave him treasures of gold, frankincense, and myrrh. But God warned the wise men in a dream not to go back to Herod. So they went home to their own country a different way.[14]

1.12 Jesus' Family Escapes to Egypt

After the wise men left, an angel from the Lord came to Joseph in a dream. The angel said, "Get up! Take the child with his mother and escape to Egypt. Herod wants to kill the child and will soon start looking for him. Stay in Egypt until I tell you to come back."

So Joseph got ready and left for Egypt with the child and the mother. They left during the night. Joseph stayed in Egypt until Herod died. This gave full meaning to what the Lord said through the prophet: "I called my son to come out of Egypt."[15]

1.13 The Killing of the Baby Boys in Bethlehem

Herod saw that the wise men had fooled him, and he was very angry. So he gave an order to kill all the baby boys in Bethlehem and the whole area around Bethlehem. Herod had learned from the wise men the time the baby was born. It was now two years from that time. So he said to kill all the boys who were two years old and younger. This gave full meaning to what God said through the prophet Jeremiah:

"A sound was heard in Ramah—
 bitter crying and great sadness.
Rachel cries for her children,
 and she cannot be comforted, because her children are gone."[16]

1.14 Jesus' Family Returns From Egypt

While Joseph was in Egypt, Herod died. An angel from the Lord came to Joseph in a dream and said, "Get up! Take the child with his mother and go to Israel. Those who were trying to kill the child are now dead."

So Joseph took the child and the mother and went to Israel. But he heard that Archelaus was now king in Judea. Archelaus became king when his father Herod died. So Joseph was afraid to go there. Then, after being warned in a dream, he went away to the area of Galilee. He went to a town called Nazareth and lived there. This gave full meaning to what God said through the prophets. God said the Messiah would be called a Nazarene.[17]

The little boy Jesus was developing into a mature young man, full of wisdom. God was blessing him.

1.15 The Boy Jesus at the Temple

Every year Jesus' parents went to Jerusalem for the Passover festival. When Jesus was twelve years old, they went to the festival as usual. When the festival was over, they went home, but Jesus stayed in Jerusalem. His parents did not know about it. They traveled for a whole day thinking that Jesus was with them in the group. They began looking for him among their family and close friends, but they did not find him. So they went back to Jerusalem to look for him there.

After three days they found him. Jesus was sitting in the Temple area with the religious teachers, listening and asking them questions. Everyone who heard him was amazed at his understanding and wise answers. When his parents saw him, they wondered how this was possible. And his mother said, "Son, why did you do this to us? Your father and I were very worried about you. We have been looking for you."

Jesus said to them, "Why did you have to look for me? You should have known that I must be where my Father's work is." But they did not understand the meaning of what he said to them.

Jesus went with them to Nazareth and obeyed them. His mother was still thinking about all these things. As Jesus grew taller, he continued to grow in wisdom. God was pleased with him and so were the people who knew him.[18]

2 Jesus' Public Life

2.1 John the Baptizer Prepares the Way for Jesus

It was the 15th year of the rule of Tiberius Caesar. These men were under Caesar: Pontius Pilate, the governor of Judea; Herod, the ruler of Galilee; Philip, Herod's brother, the ruler of Iturea and Trachonitis; Lysanias, the ruler of Abilene. Annas and Caiaphas were the high priests.

During this time, John, the son of Zechariah, was living in the desert, and he received a message from God. So he went through the whole area around the Jordan River and told the people God's message. He told them to be baptized to show that they wanted to change their lives, and then their sins would be forgiven. This is like the words written in the book of Isaiah the prophet:

"There is someone shouting in the desert:
'Prepare the way for the Lord.
 Make the road straight for him.
 Every valley will be filled,
  and every mountain and hill will be made flat.
 Crooked roads will be made straight,
  and rough roads will be made smooth.
 Then everyone will see how God will save his people!'"[19]

John's clothes were made from camel's hair, and he had a leather belt around his waist. For food, he ate locusts and wild honey. People came to John from Jerusalem and the rest of Judea and from all the areas along the Jordan River. They confessed the bad things they had done, and John baptized them in the Jordan.

Many Pharisees and Sadducees came to where John was baptizing people. When John saw them, he said, "You are all snakes! Who warned you to run from God's judgment that is coming? Change your hearts!

And show by the way you live that you have changed. I know what you are thinking. You want to say, 'but Abraham is our father!' That means nothing. I tell you, God could make children for Abraham from these rocks. The ax is now ready to cut down the trees. Every tree that does not produce good fruit will be cut down and thrown into the fire.[20]

The people asked John, "What should we do?"

He answered, "If you have two shirts, share with someone who does not have one. If you have food, share that too."

Even the tax collectors came to John. They wanted to be baptized. They said to him, "Teacher, what should we do?"

He told them, "Don't take more taxes from people than you have been ordered to collect."

The soldiers asked him, "What about us? What should we do?"

He said to them, "Don't use force or lies to make people give you money. Be happy with the pay you get."

Everyone was hoping for the Messiah to come, and they wondered about John. They thought, "Maybe he is the Messiah."

John's answer to this was, "I baptize you in water, but there is someone coming later who is able to do more than I can. I am not good enough to be the slave who unties his sandals. He will baptize you with the Holy Spirit and with fire. He will come ready to clean the grain. He will separate the good grain from the straw, and he will put the good part into his barn. Then he will burn the useless part with a fire that cannot be stopped." John said many other things like this to encourage the people to change, and he told them the Good News.[21]

2.2 The Baptism of Jesus

Then Jesus came from Galilee to the Jordan River. He came to John, wanting John to baptize him. But John tried to stop him. John said, "Why do you come to me to be baptized? I should be baptized by you!"

Jesus answered, "Let it be this way for now. We should do whatever God says is right." Then John agreed.

So Jesus was baptized. As soon as he came up out of the water, the sky opened, and he saw God's Spirit coming down on him like a dove. A voice from heaven said, "This is my Son, the one I love. I am very pleased with him."[22]

When Jesus began to teach, he was about 30 years old.[23]

2.3 The Temptation of Jesus

Then the Spirit led Jesus into the desert. He was taken there to be tempted by the devil. Jesus ate nothing for 40 days and nights. After this, he was very hungry. The devil came to tempt him and said, "If you are the Son of God, tell these rocks to become bread."

Jesus answered him, "The Scriptures say,

'It is not just bread that keeps people alive.
  Their lives depend on what God says.'"

Then the devil led Jesus to the holy city of Jerusalem and put him on a high place at the edge of the Temple area. He said to Jesus, "If you are the Son of God, jump off, because the Scriptures say,

'God will command his angels to help you,
  and their hands will catch you,
 so that you will not hit your foot on a rock.'"

Jesus answered, "The Scriptures also say,

'You must not test the Lord your God.'"

Then the devil led Jesus to the top of a very high mountain and showed him all the kingdoms of the world and all the wonderful things in them. The devil said, "If you will bow down and worship me, I will give you all these things."

Jesus said to him, "Get away from me, Satan! The Scriptures say,

'You must worship the Lord your God.
  Serve only him!'"

So the devil left him. Then some angels came to Jesus and helped him.[24]

2.4 John the Baptizer Tells About the Messiah

The Jewish leaders in Jerusalem sent some priests and Levites to John to ask him, "Who are you?" He told them the truth. Without any hesitation he said openly and plainly, "I am not the Messiah."

They asked him, "Then who are you? Are you Elijah?"
He answered, "No, I am not Elijah."
They asked, "Are you the Prophet?"
He answered, "No, I am not the Prophet."

Then they said, "Who are you? Tell us about yourself. Give us an answer to tell the people who sent us. What do you say about yourself?"

John told them the words of the prophet Isaiah:

"I am the voice of someone shouting in the desert:
   'Make a straight road ready for the Lord.'"

These Jews were sent from the Pharisees. They said to John, "You say you are not the Messiah. You say you are not Elijah or the Prophet. Then why do you baptize people?"

John answered, "I baptize people with water. But there is someone here with you that you don't know. He is the one who is coming later. I am not good enough to be the slave who unties the strings on his sandals."

These things all happened at Bethany on the other side of the Jordan River. This is where John was baptizing people.[25]

2.5 Jesus, the Lamb of God

The next day John saw Jesus coming toward him and said, "Look, the Lamb of God. He takes away the sins of the world! This is the one I was talking about when I said, 'There is a man coming after me who is greater than I am, because he was living even before I was born.' I did not know who he was. But I came baptizing people with water so that Israel could know that Jesus is the Messiah."

Then John said, "I also did not know who the Messiah was. But the one who sent me to baptize with water told me, 'You will see the Spirit come down and rest on a man. He is the one who will baptize with the Holy Spirit.' I have seen this happen. I saw the Spirit come down from heaven like a dove and rest on this man. So this is what I tell people: 'He is the Son of God.'"[26]

2.6 John Introduces His Followers to Jesus

The next day John was there again and had two of his followers with him. He saw Jesus walking by and said, "Look, the Lamb of God!"

The two followers heard him say this, so they followed Jesus. Jesus turned and saw the two men following him. He asked, "What do you want?"

They said, "Rabbi, where are you staying?" ("Rabbi" means "Teacher.")

He answered, "Come with me and you will see." So the two men went with him. They saw the place where he was staying, and they stayed there with him that day. It was about four o'clock.

These men followed Jesus after they had heard about him from John. One of them was Andrew, the brother of Simon Peter. The first thing Andrew did was to go and find his brother Simon. Andrew said to him, "We have found the Messiah." ("Messiah" means "Christ.")

Then Andrew brought Simon to Jesus. Jesus looked at him and said, "You are Simon, the son of John. You will be called Cephas." ("Cephas" means "Peter.")[27]

2.7 Jesus Calls Phillip and Nathanael

The next day Jesus decided to go to Galilee. He met Philip and said to him, "Follow me." Philip was from the town of Bethsaida, the same as Andrew and Peter. Philip found Nathanael and told him, "We have found the man that Moses wrote about in the law. The prophets wrote about him too. He is Jesus, the son of Joseph. He is from Nazareth."

But Nathanael said to Philip, "Nazareth! Can anything good come from Nazareth?"

Philip answered, "Come and see."

Jesus saw Nathanael coming toward him and said, "This man coming is a true Israelite, one you can trust."

Nathanael asked, "How do you know me?"

Jesus answered, "I saw you when you were under the fig tree, before Philip told you about me."

Then Nathanael said, "Teacher, you are the Son of God. You are the King of Israel."

Jesus said to him, "Do you believe this just because I said I saw you under the fig tree? You will see much greater things than that!" Then he said, "Believe me when I say that you will all see heaven open. You will see 'angels of God going up and coming down' on the Son of Man."[28]

2.8 Jesus' First Miraculous Sign

Two days later there was a wedding in the town of Cana in Galilee, and Jesus' mother was there. Jesus and his followers were also invited. At the wedding there was not enough wine, so Jesus' mother said to him, "They have no more wine."

Jesus answered, "Dear woman, why are you telling me this? It is not yet time for me to begin my work."

His mother said to the servants, "Do what he tells you."

There were six large stone waterpots there that were used by the Jews in their washing ceremonies. Each one held about 20 or 30 gallons.

Jesus said to the servants, "Fill the waterpots with water." So they filled them to the top.

Then he said to them, "Now dip out some water and take it to the man in charge of the feast."

So they did what he said. Then the man in charge tasted it, but the water had become wine. He did not know where the wine had come from, but the servants who brought the water knew. He called the bridegroom and said to him, "People always serve the best wine first. Later, when the guests are drunk, they serve the cheaper wine. But you have saved the best wine until now."

This was the first of all the miraculous signs Jesus did. He did it in the town of Cana in Galilee. By this he showed his divine greatness, and his followers believed in him.

Then Jesus went to the town of Capernaum. His mother and brothers and his followers went with him. They all stayed there a few days.[29]

2.9 Jesus at the Temple

It was almost time for the Jewish Passover, so Jesus went to Jerusalem. There in the Temple area he saw men selling cattle, sheep, and doves. He saw others sitting at tables, exchanging and trading people's money. Jesus made a whip with some pieces of rope. Then he forced all these men and the sheep and cattle to leave the Temple area. He turned over the tables of the money traders and scattered their money. Then he said to those who were selling pigeons, "Take these things out of here! Don't make my Father's house a place for buying and selling!"

When this happened, his followers remembered what was written in the Scriptures:

The Life and Teachings of Jesus of Nazareth

"My strong devotion to your Temple will destroy me."

Some Jews said to Jesus, "Show us a miracle as a sign from God. Prove that you have the right to do these things."

Jesus answered, "Destroy this temple and I will build it again in three days."

They answered, "People worked 46 years to build this Temple! Do you really believe you can build it again in three days?"

But the temple Jesus meant was his own body. After he was raised from death, his followers remembered that he had said this. So they believed the Scriptures, and they believed the words Jesus said.

Jesus was in Jerusalem for the Passover festival. Many people believed in him because they saw the miraculous signs he did. But Jesus did not trust them, because he knew how all people think. He did not need anyone to tell him what a person was like. He already knew.[30]

2.10 Jesus and Nicodemus

There was a man named Nicodemus, one of the Pharisees. He was an important Jewish leader. One night he came to Jesus and said, "Teacher, we know that you are a teacher sent from God. No one can do these miraculous signs that you do unless they have God's help."

Jesus answered, "I assure you, everyone must be born again. Anyone who is not born again cannot be in God's kingdom."

Nicodemus said, "How can a man who is already old be born again? Can he go back into his mother's womb and be born a second time?"

Jesus answered, "Believe me when I say that everyone must be born from water and the Spirit. Anyone who is not born from water and the Spirit cannot enter God's kingdom. The only life people get from their human parents is physical. But the new life that the Spirit gives a person is spiritual. Don't be surprised that I told you, 'You must be born again.' The wind blows wherever it wants to. You hear it, but you don't know where it is coming from or where it is going. It is the same with everyone who is born from the Spirit."

Nicodemus asked, "How is all this possible?"

Jesus said, "You are an important teacher of Israel, and you still don't understand these things? The truth is, we talk about what we know. We tell about what we have seen. But you people don't accept what we tell you. I have told you about things here on earth, but you do not believe me. So I'm sure you will not believe me if I tell you about heavenly things! The only one who has ever gone up to heaven is the one who came down from heaven—the Son of Man.

"Moses lifted up the snake in the desert. It is the same with the Son of Man. He must be lifted up too. Then everyone who believes in him can have eternal life."

Yes, God loved the world so much that he gave his only Son, so that everyone who believes in him would not be lost but have eternal life. God sent his Son into the world. He did not send him to judge the world guilty, but to save the world through him. People who believe in God's Son are not judged guilty. But people who do not believe are already judged, because they have not believed in God's only Son. They are judged by this fact: The light has come into the world. But they did not want light. They wanted darkness, because they were doing evil things. Everyone who does evil hates the light. They will not come to the light, because the light will show all the bad things they have done. But anyone who follows the true way comes to the light. Then the light will show that whatever they have done was done through God.[31]

2.11 Jesus and John the Baptizer

After this, Jesus and his followers went into the area of Judea. There he stayed with his followers and baptized people. John was also baptizing people in Aenon, a place near Salim with plenty of water. People were going there to be baptized. This was before John was put in prison.

Some of John's followers had an argument with another Jew about religious washing. Then they came to John and said, "Teacher, remember the man who was with you on the other side of the Jordan River? He is the one you were telling everyone about. He is also baptizing people, and many are going to him."

John answered, "A person can receive only what God gives. You yourselves heard me say, 'I am not the Messiah. I am only the one God sent to prepare the way for him.' The bride always belongs to the bridegroom. The friend who helps the bridegroom just waits and listens. He is happy just to hear the bridegroom talk. That's how I feel now. I am so happy that he is here. He must become more and more important, and I must become less important.

The Life and Teachings of Jesus of Nazareth

"The one who comes from above is greater than all others. The one who is from the earth belongs to the earth. He talks about things that are on the earth. But the one who comes from heaven is greater than all others. He tells what he has seen and heard, but people don't accept what he says. Whoever accepts what he says has given proof that God speaks the truth. God sent him, and he tells people what God says. God gives him the Spirit fully. The Father loves the Son and has given him power over everything. Whoever believes in the Son has eternal life. But those who do not obey the Son will never have that life. They cannot get away from God's anger."

Jesus learned that the Pharisees had heard the report that he was making and baptizing more followers than John. (But really, Jesus himself did not baptize anyone; his followers baptized people for him.) So he left Judea and went back to Galilee.[32]

2.12 John the Baptizer Put in Prison

John criticized Herod the ruler for what he had done with Herodias, the wife of Herod's brother, as well as for all the other bad things he had done. So Herod added another bad thing to all his other wrongs: He put John in jail.[33]

When Jesus heard that John was put in prison,[34] he went back to Galilee with the power of the Spirit.[35]

2.13 Jesus Talks to a Samaritan Woman

On the way to Galilee he had to go through the country of Samaria. In Samaria Jesus came to the town called Sychar, which is near the field that Jacob gave to his son Joseph. Jacob's well was there. Jesus was tired from his long trip, so he sat down beside the well. It was about noon. A Samaritan woman came to the well to get some water, and Jesus said to her, "Please give me a drink." This happened while his followers were in town buying some food.

The woman answered, "I am surprised that you ask me for a drink! You are a Jew and I am a Samaritan woman!" (Jews have nothing to do with Samaritans.)

Jesus answered, "You don't know what God can give you. And you don't know who I am, the one who asked you for a drink. If you knew, you would have asked me, and I would have given you living water."

The woman said, "Sir, where will you get that living water? The well is very deep, and you have nothing to get water with. Are you greater than our ancestor Jacob? He is the one who gave us this well. He drank from it himself, and his sons and all his animals drank from it too."

Jesus answered, "Everyone who drinks this water will be thirsty again. But anyone who drinks the water I give will never be thirsty again. The water I give people will be like a spring flowing inside them. It will bring them eternal life."

The woman said to Jesus, "Sir, give me this water. Then I will never be thirsty again and won't have to come back here to get more water."

Jesus told her, "Go get your husband and come back."

The woman answered, "But I have no husband."

Jesus said to her, "You are right to say you have no husband. That's because, although you have had five husbands, the man you live with now is not your husband. That much was the truth."

The woman said, "Sir, I can see that you are a prophet. Our fathers worshiped on this mountain. But you Jews say that Jerusalem is the place where people must worship."

Jesus said, "Believe me, woman! The time is coming when you will not have to be in Jerusalem or on this mountain to worship the Father. You Samaritans worship something you don't understand. We Jews understand what we worship, since salvation comes from the Jews. But the time is coming when the true worshipers will worship the Father in spirit and truth. In fact, that time is now here. And these are the kind of people the Father wants to be his worshipers. God is spirit. So the people who worship him must worship in spirit and truth."

The woman said, "I know that the Messiah is coming." (Messiah is the one called Christ.) "When he comes, he will explain everything to us."

Then Jesus said, "He is talking to you now—I'm the Messiah."[36]

2.14 Jesus' Followers Return

Just then Jesus' followers came back from town. They were surprised because they saw Jesus talking with a woman. But none of them asked, "What do you want?" or "Why are you talking with her?"

Then the woman left her water jar and went back to town. She told the people there, "A man told me everything I have ever done. Come see him. Maybe he is the Messiah." So the people left the town and went to see Jesus.

While the woman was in town, Jesus' followers were begging him, "Teacher, eat something!"

But Jesus answered, "I have food to eat that you know nothing about."

So the followers asked themselves, "Did someone already bring him some food?"

Jesus said, "My food is to do what the one who sent me wants me to do. My food is to finish the work that he gave me to do. When you plant, you always say, 'Four more months to wait before we gather the grain.' But I tell you, open your eyes, and look at the fields. They are ready for harvesting now. Even now, the people who harvest the crop are being paid. They are gathering crops for eternal life. So now the people who plant can be happy together with those who harvest. It is true when we say, 'One person plants, but another person harvests the crop.' I sent you to harvest a crop that you did not work for. Others did the work, and you get the profit from their work."[37]

2.15 Many Samaritans Believe

Many of the Samaritans in that town believed in Jesus. They believed because of what the woman had told them about him. She had told them, "He told me everything I have ever done." The Samaritans went to Jesus. They begged him to stay with them. So he stayed there two days. Many more people became believers because of the things he said.

The people said to the woman, "First we believed in Jesus because of what you told us. But now we believe because we heard him ourselves. We know now that he really is the one who will save the world."[38]

2.16 Jesus Returns to Galilee

Two days later Jesus left and went to Galilee. (Jesus had said before that a prophet is not respected in his own country.) When he arrived in Galilee, the people there welcomed him. They had been at the Passover festival in Jerusalem and had seen everything he did there.[39]

2.17 Jesus Heals an Official's Son

Jesus went to visit Cana in Galilee again. Cana is where he had changed the water into wine. One of the king's important officials lived in the city of Capernaum. This man's son was sick. The man heard

Jesus' Public Life

that Jesus had come from Judea and was now in Galilee. So he went to Jesus and begged him to come to Capernaum and heal his son, who was almost dead. Jesus said to him, "You people must see miraculous signs and wonders before you will believe in me."

The king's official said, "Sir, come before my little son dies."

Jesus answered, "Go. Your son will live."

The man believed what Jesus told him and went home. On the way home the man's servants came and met him. They said, "Your son is well."

The man asked, "What time did my son begin to get well?"

They answered, "It was about one o'clock yesterday when the fever left him."

The father knew that one o'clock was the same time that Jesus had said, "Your son will live." So the man and everyone in his house believed in Jesus.

That was the second miraculous sign that Jesus did after coming from Judea to Galilee.[40]

2.18 Jesus Rejected in His Hometown

Jesus traveled to Nazareth, the town where he grew up. On the Sabbath day he went to the synagogue as he always did. He stood up to read. The book of Isaiah the prophet was given to him. He opened the book and found the place where this is written:

"The Spirit of the Lord is on me.
 He has chosen me to tell good news to the poor.
 He sent me to tell prisoners that they are free
   and to tell the blind that they can see again.
 He sent me to free those who have been treated badly
   and to announce that the time has come for the Lord to show his kindness."

Jesus closed the book, gave it back to the helper, and sat down. As everyone in the synagogue watched him closely, he began to speak to them. He said, "While you heard me reading these words just now, they were coming true!"

Everyone there said good things about Jesus. They were amazed to hear him speak such wonderful words. They said, "How is this possible? Isn't he Joseph's son?"

Jesus said to them, "I know you will tell me the old saying: 'Doctor, heal yourself.' You want to say, 'We heard about the things you did in Capernaum. Do those same things here in your own hometown!'" Then he said, "The truth is, a prophet is not accepted in his own hometown.

"During the time of Elijah it did not rain in Israel for three and a half years. There was no food anywhere in the whole country. There were many widows in Israel during that time. But the fact is, Elijah was sent to none of those widows in Israel. He was sent only to a widow in Zarephath, a town in Sidon.

"And there were many people with leprosy living in Israel during the time of the prophet Elisha. But none of them were healed; the only one was Naaman. And he was from the country of Syria, not Israel."

When the people in the synagogue heard this, they were very angry. They got up and forced Jesus to go out of town. Their town was built on a hill. They took Jesus to the edge of the hill to throw him off. But he walked through the middle of the crowd and went away.[41]

2.19 Jesus Begins Telling People the Good News

But he did not stay in Nazareth. He went to live in Capernaum, a town near Lake Galilee in the area near Zebulun and Naphtali. He did this to give full meaning to what the prophet Isaiah said:

"Listen, land of Zebulun and land of Naphtali,
    lands by the road that goes to the sea, the area past the Jordan River—
    Galilee, where those from other nations live.
The people who live in spiritual darkness
    have seen a great light.
The light has shined for those
    who live in the land that is as dark as a grave."

From that time Jesus began to tell[42] people the Good News from God. He said, "The right time is now here. God's kingdom is near. Change your hearts and lives, and believe the Good News!"[43] Stories about him spread all over the area around Galilee. He began to teach in the synagogues, and everyone praised him.[44]

3 The Year of Popularity

3.1 Jesus Chooses Some Followers

As Jesus was walking by Lake Galilee, he saw two brothers, Simon (called Peter) and Simon's brother Andrew. These brothers were fishermen, and they were fishing in the lake with a net. Jesus said to them, "Come, follow me, and I will make you a different kind of fishermen. You will bring in people, not fish." Simon and Andrew immediately left their nets and followed him.

Jesus continued walking by Lake Galilee. He saw two other brothers, James and John, the sons of Zebedee. They were in a boat with their father Zebedee. They were preparing their nets to catch fish. Jesus told the brothers to come with him. So they immediately left the boat and their father, and they followed Jesus.[45]

As Jesus stood beside Lake Galilee, a crowd of people pushed to get closer to him and to hear the teachings of God. Jesus saw two boats at the shore of the lake. The fishermen were washing their nets. Jesus got into the boat that belonged to Simon. He asked Simon to push off a little from the shore. Then he sat down in the boat and taught the people on the shore.

When Jesus finished speaking, he said to Simon, "Take the boat into the deep water. If all of you will put your nets into the water, you will catch some fish."

Simon answered, "Master, we worked hard all night trying to catch fish and caught nothing. But you say I should put the nets into the water, so I will." The fishermen put their nets into the water. Their nets were filled with so many fish that they began to break. They called to their friends in the other boat to come and help them. The friends came, and both boats were filled so full of fish that they were almost sinking.

The fishermen were all amazed at the many fish they caught. When Simon Peter saw this, he bowed down before Jesus and said, "Go

The Life and Teachings of Jesus of Nazareth

away from me, Lord. I am a sinful man!" James and John, the sons of Zebedee, were amazed too. (James and John worked together with Simon.)

Jesus said to Simon, "Don't be afraid. From now on your work will be to bring in people, not fish!"

The men brought their boats to the shore. They left everything and followed Jesus.[46]

3.2 Jesus Frees a Man From an Evil Spirit

Jesus and his followers went to Capernaum. On the Sabbath day, Jesus went into the synagogue and taught the people. They were amazed at his teaching. He did not teach like their teachers of the law. He taught like someone with authority. While Jesus was in the synagogue, a man was there who had an evil spirit inside him. The man shouted, "Jesus of Nazareth! What do you want with us? Did you come to destroy us? I know who you are—God's Holy One!"

Jesus, his voice full of warning, said, "Be quiet, and come out of him!" The evil spirit made the man shake. Then the spirit made a loud noise and came out of him.

The people were amazed. They asked each other, "What is happening here? This man is teaching something new, and he teaches with authority! He even commands evil spirits, and they obey him." So the news about Jesus spread quickly everywhere in the area of Galilee.[47]

3.3 Jesus Heals Many People

Jesus and the followers left the synagogue. They all went with James and John to the home of Simon and Andrew. Simon's mother-in-law was very sick. She was in bed and had a fever. The people there told Jesus about her. So he went to her bed. Jesus held her hand and helped her stand up. The fever left her, and she was healed. Then she began serving them.

That night, after the sun went down, the people brought to Jesus many who were sick. They also brought those who had demons inside them. Everyone in the town gathered at the door of that house. Jesus healed many of those who had different kinds of sicknesses. He also forced many demons out of people. But he would not allow the demons to speak, because they knew who he was.[48]

3.4 Jesus Prays Alone

The next morning Jesus woke up very early. He left the house while it was still dark and went to a place where he could be alone and pray. Later, Simon and his friends went to look for Jesus. They found him and said, "Everyone is looking for you!"

Jesus answered, "We should go to another place. We can go to other towns around here, and I can tell God's message to those people too. That is why I came."[49]

3.5 Jesus Teaches and Heals the People

Jesus went everywhere in the country of Galilee. He taught in the synagogues and told the Good News about God's kingdom. And he healed all the people's diseases and sicknesses. The news about Jesus spread all over Syria, and people brought to him all those who were sick. They were suffering from different kinds of diseases and pain. Some had demons inside them, some suffered from seizures, and some were paralyzed. Jesus healed them all. Large crowds followed him—people from Galilee, the Ten Towns, Jerusalem, Judea, and the area across the Jordan River.[50]

3.6 Jesus Heals a Sick Man

A man who had leprosy came to Jesus. The man bowed on his knees and begged him, "You have the power to heal me if you want."

Jesus felt sorry for the man. So he touched him and said, "I want to heal you. Be healed!" Immediately the leprosy disappeared, and the man was healed.

Jesus told the man to go, but he gave him a strong warning: "Don't tell anyone about what I did for you. But go and show yourself to the priest. And offer a gift to God because you have been healed. Offer the gift that Moses commanded. This will show everyone that you are healed." The man left there and told everyone he saw that Jesus had healed him. So the news about Jesus spread. And that is why he could not enter a town if people saw him. He stayed in places where people did not live. But people came from all the towns to the places where he was.[51]

3.7 Jesus Heals a Crippled Man

A few days later, Jesus came back to Capernaum. The news spread that he was back home. A large crowd gathered to hear him speak. The house was so full that there was no place to stand, not even outside the door. While Jesus was teaching, some people brought a paralyzed man to see him. He was being carried by four of them. But they could not get the man inside to Jesus because the house was so full of people. So they went to the roof above Jesus and made a hole in it. Then they lowered the mat with the paralyzed man on it. When Jesus saw how much faith they had, he said to the paralyzed man, "Young man, your sins are forgiven."

Some of the teachers of the law were sitting there. They saw what Jesus did, and they said to themselves, "Why does this man say things like that? What an insult to God! No one but God can forgive sins."

Jesus knew immediately what these teachers of the law were thinking. So he said to them, "Why do you have these questions in your minds? The Son of Man has power on earth to forgive sins. But how can I prove this to you? Maybe you are thinking it was easy for me to say to the crippled man, 'Your sins are forgiven.' There's no proof it really happened. But what if I say to the man, 'Stand up. Take your mat and walk'? Then you will be able to see if I really have this power or not." So Jesus said to the paralyzed man, "I tell you, stand up. Take your mat and go home."

Immediately the paralyzed man stood up. He picked up his mat and walked out of the room. Everyone could see him. They were amazed and praised God. They said, "This is the most amazing thing we have ever seen!"[52]

3.8 Levi Follows Jesus

Jesus went to the lake again, and many people followed him there. So Jesus taught them. He was walking beside the lake, and he saw a man named Levi, son of Alphaeus. Levi was sitting at his place for collecting taxes. Jesus said to him, "Follow me." Then Levi stood up and followed Jesus.

Later that day, Jesus and his followers ate at Levi's house. There were also many tax collectors and others with bad reputations eating with them. (There were many of these people who followed Jesus.) When some teachers of the law who were Pharisees saw Jesus eating with such bad people, they asked his followers, "Why does he eat with tax collectors and sinners?"

When Jesus heard this, he said to them, "It is the sick people who need a doctor, not those who are healthy. I did not come to invite good people. I came to invite sinners."[53]

3.9 Jesus Answers a Question About Fasting

They said to Jesus, "John's followers often fast and pray, the same as the followers of the Pharisees. But your followers eat and drink all the time."

Jesus said to them, "At a wedding you can't ask the friends of the bridegroom to be sad and fast while he is still with them. But the time will come when the groom will be taken away from them. Then his friends will fast."

Jesus told them this story: "No one takes cloth off a new coat to cover a hole in an old coat. That would ruin the new coat, and the cloth from the new coat would not be the same as the old cloth. Also, no one ever pours new wine into old wineskins. The new wine would break them. The wine would spill out, and the wineskins would be ruined. You always put new wine into new wineskins. No one who drinks old wine wants new wine. They say, 'The old wine is just fine.'"[54]

3.10 Jesus Heals a Man at a Pool

Later, Jesus went to Jerusalem for a special Jewish festival. In Jerusalem there is a pool with five covered porches. In Aramaic it is called Bethzatha. This pool is near the Sheep Gate. Many sick people were lying on the porches beside the pool. Some of them were blind, some were crippled, and some were paralyzed. One of the men lying there had been sick for 38 years. Jesus saw him lying there and knew that he had been sick for a very long time. So he asked him, "Do you want to be well?"

The sick man answered, "Sir, there is no one to help me get into the water when it starts moving. I try to be the first one into the water. But when I try, someone else always goes in before I can."

Then Jesus said, "Stand up! Pick up your mat and walk." Immediately the man was well. He picked up his mat and started walking.

The day all this happened was a Sabbath day. So some Jews said to the man who had been healed, "Today is the Sabbath. It is against our law for you to carry your mat on the Sabbath day."

But he answered, "The man who made me well told me, 'Pick up your mat and walk.'"

They asked him, "Who is the man who told you to pick up your mat and walk?"

But the man who had been healed did not know who it was. There were many people there, and Jesus had left.

Later, Jesus found the man at the Temple and said to him, "See, you are well now. But stop sinning or something worse may happen to you!"

Then the man left and went back to the Jews who questioned him. He told them that Jesus was the one who made him well.

Jesus was doing all this on the Sabbath day. So these Jews began trying to make him stop. But he said to them, "My Father never stops working, and so I work too."

This made them try harder to kill him. They said, "First this man was breaking the law about the Sabbath day. Then he said that God is his Father! He is making himself equal with God!"[55]

3.11 *The Son Gives Life*

But Jesus answered, "I assure you that the Son can do nothing alone. He does only what he sees his Father doing. The Son does the same things that the Father does. The Father loves the Son and shows him everything he does. This man was healed. But the Father will show the Son greater things than this to do. Then you will all be amazed. The Father raises the dead and gives them life. In the same way, the Son gives life to those he wants to.

"Also, the Father judges no one. He has given the Son power to do all the judging. God did this so that all people will respect the Son the same as they respect the Father. Anyone who does not respect the Son does not respect the Father. He is the one who sent the Son.

"I assure you, anyone who hears what I say and believes in the one who sent me has eternal life. They will not be judged guilty. They have already left death and have entered into life. Believe me, an important time is coming. That time is already here. People who are dead will hear the voice of the Son of God. And those who listen will live. Life comes from the Father himself. So the Father has also allowed the Son to give life. And the Father has given him the power to judge all people because he is the Son of Man.

"Don't be surprised at this. A time is coming when all people who are dead and in their graves will hear his voice. Then they will come out of their graves. Those who did good in this life will rise and have eternal life. But those who did evil will rise to be judged guilty.

"I can do nothing alone. I judge only the way I am told. And my judgment is right, because I am not trying to please myself. I want only to please the one who sent me."[56]

3.12 Jesus Gives Proofs of His Authority

"If I tell people about myself, they cannot be sure that what I say is true. But there is someone else who tells people about me, and I know that what he says about me is true.

"You sent men to John, and he told you what is true. I don't need anyone to tell people about me, but I remind you of what John said so that you can be saved. John was like a lamp that burned and gave light, and you were happy to enjoy his light for a while.

"But I have a proof about myself that is greater than anything John said. The things I do are my proof. These are what my Father gave me to do. They show that the Father sent me. And the Father who sent me has given proof about me himself. But you have never heard his voice. You have never seen what he looks like. The Father's teaching does not live in you, because you don't believe in the one the Father sent. You carefully study the Scriptures. You think that they give you eternal life. These same Scriptures tell about me! But you refuse to come to me to have that life.

"I don't want praise from you or any other human. But I know you—I know that you have no love for God. I have come from my Father and speak for him, but you don't accept me. But when other people come speaking only for themselves, you accept them. You like to have praise from each other. But you never try to get the praise that comes from the only God. So how can you believe? Don't think that I will be the one to stand before the Father and accuse you. Moses is the one to accuse you. And he is the one you hoped would save you. If you really believed Moses, you would believe me, because he wrote about me. But you don't believe what he wrote, so you can't believe what I say."[57]

3.13 Jesus Is Lord Over the Sabbath Day

On the Sabbath day, Jesus and his followers were walking through some grain fields. The followers picked some grain to eat. Some Pharisees said to Jesus, "Why are your followers doing this? It is against the law to pick grain on the Sabbath."

Jesus answered, "You have read what David did when he and the people with him were hungry and needed food. It was during the time of Abiathar the high priest. David went into God's house and ate the bread that was offered to God. And the Law of Moses says that only priests can eat that bread. David also gave some of the bread to the people with him."[58]

And you have read in the Law of Moses that on every Sabbath day the priests at the Temple break the law about the Sabbath day. But they are not wrong for doing that. I tell you that there is something here that is greater than the Temple. The Scriptures say, 'I don't want animal sacrifices; I want you to show kindness to people.' You don't really know what that means. If you understood it, you would not judge those who have done nothing wrong.[59]

Then Jesus said to the Pharisees, "The Sabbath day was made to help people. People were not made to be ruled by the Sabbath. So the Son of Man is Lord of every day, even the Sabbath."[60]

Jesus went from there to their synagogue. In the synagogue there was a man with a crippled hand. Some Jews there were looking for a reason to accuse Jesus of doing wrong. So they asked him, "Is it right to heal on the Sabbath day?"

Jesus answered, "If any of you has a sheep and it falls into a ditch on the Sabbath day, you will take the sheep and help it out of the ditch. Surely a man is more important than a sheep. So it is right to do good on the Sabbath day."

Then Jesus said to the man with the crippled hand, "Hold out your hand." The man held out his hand, and it became well again, the same as the other hand. But the Pharisees left and made plans to kill Jesus.[61]

3.14 A Large Crowd Follows Jesus

Jesus went away with his followers to the lake. A large crowd of people from Galilee followed them. Many also came from Judea, from Jerusalem, from Idumea, from the area across the Jordan River, and from the area around Tyre and Sidon. These people came because they heard about all that Jesus was doing.

Jesus saw how many people there were, so he told his followers to get a small boat and make it ready for him. He wanted the boat so that the crowds of people could not push against him. He had healed many of them, so all the sick people were pushing toward him to touch him. Some people had evil spirits inside them. When the evil spirits saw Jesus, they bowed before him and shouted, "You are the Son of God!" But Jesus gave the spirits a strong warning not to tell anyone who he was.[62]

This was to give full meaning to what Isaiah the prophet said when he spoke for God:

"Here is my servant,
 the one I have chosen.
He is the one I love,
 and I am very pleased with him.
I will fill him with my Spirit,
 and he will bring justice to the nations.
He will not argue or shout;
 no one will hear his voice in the streets.
He will not break off even a bent stem of grass.
 He will not put out even the weakest flame.
 He will not give up until he has made justice victorious.
All people will hope in him."[63]

Jesus and the apostles came down from the mountain. Jesus stood on a flat place. A large crowd of his followers was there. Also, there were many people from all around Judea, Jerusalem, and the seacoast cities of Tyre and Sidon. They all came to hear Jesus teach and to be healed of their sicknesses. He healed the people who were troubled by evil spirits. Everyone was trying to touch him, because power was coming out from him. Jesus healed them all.[64]

3.15 Jesus Chooses Twelve Apostles

A few days later, Jesus went out to a mountain to pray. He stayed there all night praying to God. The next morning he called his followers. He chose twelve and called them apostles.[65] He wanted these twelve men to be with him, and he wanted to send them to other places to tell people God's message. He also wanted them to have the power to force demons out of people. These are the names of the twelve men Jesus chose: Simon (the one Jesus named Peter), James and his brother John, the sons of Zebedee (the ones Jesus named Boanerges, which means "Sons of Thunder"), Andrew, Philip, Bartholomew, Matthew, Thomas, James, the son of Alphaeus, Thaddaeus, Simon, the Zealot, Judas Iscariot (the one who handed Jesus over to his enemies).[66]

The Sermon on the Mount (3.16-34)

3.16 *The People Who Receive God's Blessings*

When Jesus saw the crowds of people there, he went up on a hill and sat down. His followers came and sat next to him. Then Jesus began teaching the people. He said,

"Great blessings belong to those who know they are spiritually in
    need.
  God's kingdom belongs to them.
Great blessings belong to those who are sad now.
  God will comfort them.
Great blessings belong to those who are humble.
  They will be given the land God promised.
Great blessings belong to those who want to do right more than
    anything else.
  God will fully satisfy them.
Great blessings belong to those who show mercy to others.
  Mercy will be given to them.
Great blessings belong to those whose thoughts are pure.
  They will be with God.
Great blessings belong to those who work to bring peace.
  God will call them his sons and daughters.
Great blessings belong to those who suffer persecution for doing
    what is right.
  God's kingdom belongs to them.

"People will insult you and hurt you. They will lie and say all kinds of evil things about you because you follow me. But when they do that, know that great blessings belong to you. Be happy about it. Be very glad because you have a great reward waiting for you in heaven. People did these same bad things to the prophets who lived before you."67

3.17 Jesus Calls His Followers Salt and Light

"You are the salt of the earth. But if the salt loses its taste, it cannot be made salty again. Salt is useless if it loses its salty taste. It will be thrown out where people will just walk on it.

"You are the light that shines for the world to see. You are like a city built on a hill that cannot be hidden. People don't hide a lamp under a bowl. They put it on a lampstand. Then the light shines for everyone in the house. In the same way, you should be a light for other people. Live so that they will see the good things you do and praise your Father in heaven."68

3.18 Jesus and the Law of Moses

"Don't think that I have come to destroy the Law of Moses or the teaching of the prophets. I have come not to destroy their teachings but to give full meaning to them. I assure you that nothing will disappear from the law until heaven and earth are gone. The law will not lose even the smallest letter or the smallest part of a letter until it has all been done.

"A person should obey every command in the law, even one that does not seem important. Whoever refuses to obey any command and teaches others not to obey it will be the least important in God's kingdom. But whoever obeys the law and teaches others to obey it will be great in God's kingdom. I tell you that you must do better than the teachers of the law and the Pharisees. If you are not more pleasing to God than they are, you will never enter God's kingdom."69

3.19 Jesus Teaches About Anger

"You have heard that it was said to our people long ago, 'You must not murder anyone. Any person who commits murder will be judged.' But I tell you, don't be angry with anyone. If you are angry with others, you will be judged. And if you insult someone, you will be judged by the high court. And if you call someone a fool, you will be in danger of the fire of hell.

"So, what if you are offering your gift at the altar and remember that someone has something against you? Leave your gift there and go make peace with that person. Then come and offer your gift.

"If anyone wants to take you to court, make friends with them quickly. Try to do that before you get to the court. If you don't, they might hand you over to the judge. And the judge will hand you over to a guard, who will throw you into jail. I assure you that you will not leave there until you have paid everything you owe."[70]

3.20 Jesus Teaches About Adultery

"You have heard that it was said, 'You must not commit adultery.' But I tell you that if a man looks at a woman and wants to sin sexually with her, he has already committed that sin with her in his mind. If your right eye makes you sin, take it out and throw it away. It is better to lose one part of your body than to have your whole body thrown into hell. If your right hand makes you sin, cut it off and throw it away. It is better to lose one part of your body than for your whole body to go into hell."[71]

3.21 Jesus Teaches About Divorce

"It was also said, 'Any man who divorces his wife must give her a written notice of divorce.' But I tell you that any man who divorces his wife, except for the problem of sexual sin, is causing his wife to be guilty of adultery. And whoever marries a divorced woman is guilty of adultery."[72]

3.22 Jesus Teaches About Making Promises

"You have heard that it was said to our people long ago, 'When you make a vow, you must not break your promise. Keep the vows that you make to the Lord.' But I tell you, when you make a promise, don't try to make it stronger with a vow. Don't make a vow using the name of heaven, because heaven is God's throne. Don't make a vow using the name of the earth, because the earth belongs to him. Don't make a vow using the name of Jerusalem, because it also belongs to him, the great King. And don't even say that your own head is proof that you will keep your promise. You cannot make one hair on your head white or black. Say only 'yes' if you mean 'yes,' and say only 'no' if you mean 'no.' If you say more than that, it is from the Evil One."[73]

3.23 Jesus Teaches About Fighting Back

"You have heard that it was said, 'An eye for an eye, and a tooth for a tooth.' But I tell you, don't fight back against someone who wants to do harm to you. If they hit you on the right cheek, let them hit the other cheek too. If anyone wants to sue you in court and take your shirt, let them have your coat too. If a soldier forces you to walk with him one mile, go with him two. Give to anyone who asks you for something. Don't refuse to give to anyone who wants to borrow from you."[74]

3.24 Jesus Teaches About Loving Your Enemies

"You have heard that it was said, 'Love your neighbor and hate your enemy.' But I tell you, love your enemies. Pray for those who treat you badly. If you do this, you will be children who are truly like your Father in heaven. He lets the sun rise for all people, whether they are good or bad. He sends rain to those who do right and to those who do wrong. If you love only those who love you, why should you get a reward for that? Even the tax collectors do that. And if you are nice only to your friends, you are no better than anyone else. Even the people who don't know God are nice to their friends. What I am saying is that you must be perfect, just as your Father in heaven is perfect."[75]

3.25 Jesus Teaches About Giving

"Be careful! When you do something good, don't do it in front of others so that they will see you. If you do that, you will have no reward from your Father in heaven.

"When you give to those who are poor, don't announce that you are giving. Don't be like the hypocrites. When they are in the synagogues and on the streets, they blow trumpets before they give so that people will see them. They want everyone to praise them. The truth is, that's all the reward they will get. So when you give to the poor, don't let anyone know what you are doing. Your giving should be done in private. Your Father can see what is done in private, and he will reward you."[76]

3.26 Jesus Teaches About Prayer

"When you pray, don't be like the hypocrites. They love to stand in the synagogues and on the street corners and pray loudly. They want people to see them. The truth is, that's all the reward they will get. But when you pray, you should go into your room and close the door. Then pray to your Father. He is there in that private place. He can see what is done in private, and he will reward you.

"And when you pray, don't be like the people who don't know God. They say the same things again and again. They think that if they say it enough, their god will hear them. Don't be like them. Your Father knows what you need before you ask him. So this is how you should pray:

'Our Father in heaven,
  we pray that your name will always be kept holy.
We pray that your kingdom will come—
  that what you want will be done here on earth, the same as in heaven.
Give us the food we need for each day.
Forgive our sins,
  just as we have forgiven those who did wrong to us.
Don't let us be tempted,
  but save us from the Evil One.'

Yes, if you forgive others for the wrongs they do to you, then your Father in heaven will also forgive your wrongs. But if you don't forgive others, then your Father in heaven will not forgive the wrongs you do."[77]

3.27 Jesus Teaches About Fasting

"When you fast, don't make yourselves look sad like the hypocrites. They put a look of suffering on their faces so that people will see they are fasting. The truth is, that's all the reward they will get. So when you fast, wash your face and make yourself look nice. Then no one will know you are fasting, except your Father, who is with you even in private. He can see what is done in private, and he will reward you."[78]

3.28 Jesus Teaches About What Is Important

"Don't save treasures for yourselves here on earth. Moths and rust will destroy them. And thieves can break into your house and steal them. Instead, save your treasures in heaven, where they cannot be destroyed by moths or rust and where thieves cannot break in and steal them. Your heart will be where your treasure is.

"The only source of light for the body is the eye. If you look at people and want to help them, you will be full of light. But if you look at people in a selfish way, you will be full of darkness. And if the only light you have is really darkness, you have the worst kind of darkness.

"You cannot serve two masters at the same time. You will hate one and love the other, or you will be loyal to one and not care about the other. You cannot serve God and Money at the same time."[79]

3.29 Jesus Teaches About Worry

"So I tell you, don't worry about the things you need to live—what you will eat, drink, or wear. Life is more important than food, and the body is more important than what you put on it. Look at the birds. They don't plant, harvest, or save food in barns, but your heavenly Father feeds them. Don't you know you are worth much more than they are? You cannot add any time to your life by worrying about it.

"And why do you worry about clothes? Look at the wildflowers in the field. See how they grow. They don't work or make clothes for themselves. But I tell you that even Solomon, the great and rich king, was not dressed as beautifully as one of these flowers. If God makes what grows in the field so beautiful, what do you think he will do for you? It's just grass—one day it's alive, and the next day someone throws it into a fire. But God cares enough to make it beautiful. Surely he will do much more for you. Your faith is so small!

"Don't worry and say, 'What will we eat?' or 'What will we drink?' or 'What will we wear?' That's what those people who don't know God are always thinking about. Don't worry, because your Father in heaven knows that you need all these things. What you should want most is God's kingdom and doing what he wants you to do. Then he will give you all these other things you need. So don't worry about tomorrow. Each day has enough trouble of its own. Tomorrow will have its own worries."[80]

3.30 Jesus Teaches About Judging Others

"Don't judge others, and God will not judge you. If you judge others, you will be judged the same way you judge them. God will treat you the same way you treat others.

"Why do you notice the small piece of dust that is in your friend's eye, but you don't notice the big piece of wood that is in your own? Why do you say to your friend, 'Let me take that piece of dust out of your eye'? Look at yourself first! You still have that big piece of wood in your own eye. You are a hypocrite! First, take the wood out of your own eye. Then you will see clearly to get the dust out of your friend's eye.

"Don't give something that is holy to dogs. They will only turn and hurt you. And don't throw your pearls to pigs. They will only step on them."[81]

3.31 Ask God for What You Need

"Continue to ask, and God will give to you. Continue to search, and you will find. Continue to knock, and the door will open for you. Yes, whoever continues to ask will receive. Whoever continues to look will find. And whoever continues to knock will have the door opened for them.

"Do any of you have a son? If he asked for bread, would you give him a rock? Or if he asked for a fish, would you give him a snake? Of course not! You people are so bad, but you still know how to give good things to your children. So surely your heavenly Father will give good things to those who ask him.

"Do for others what you would want them to do for you. This is the meaning of the Law of Moses and the teaching of the prophets."[82]

3.32 The Narrow Gate and the Wide Gate

"You can enter true life only through the narrow gate. The gate to hell is very wide, and there is plenty of room on the road that leads there. Many people go that way. But the gate that opens the way to true life is narrow. And the road that leads there is hard to follow. Only a few people find it."[83]

3.33 What People Do Shows What They Are

"Be careful of false prophets. They come to you and look gentle like sheep. But they are really dangerous like wolves. You will know these people because of what they do. Good things don't come from people who are bad, just as grapes don't come from thornbushes, and figs don't come from thorny weeds. In the same way, every good tree produces good fruit, and bad trees produce bad fruit. A good tree cannot produce bad fruit, and a bad tree cannot produce good fruit. Every tree that does not produce good fruit is cut down and thrown into the fire. You will know these false people by what they do.

"Not everyone who calls me Lord will enter God's kingdom. The only people who will enter are those who do what my Father in heaven wants. On that last Day many will call me Lord. They will say, 'Lord, Lord, by the power of your name we spoke for God. And by your name we forced out demons and did many miracles.' Then I will tell those people clearly, 'Get away from me, you people who do wrong. I never knew you.'"[84]

3.34 Two Kinds of People

"Whoever hears these teachings of mine and obeys them is like a wise man who built his house on rock. It rained hard, the floods came, and the winds blew and beat against that house. But it did not fall because it was built on rock.

"Whoever hears these teachings of mine and does not obey them is like a foolish man who built his house on sand. It rained hard, the floods came, and the winds blew and beat against that house. And it fell with a loud crash."

When Jesus finished speaking, the people were amazed at his teaching. He did not teach like their teachers of the law. He taught like someone who has authority.

Jesus came down from the hill, and a large crowd followed him.[85]

3.35 Jesus Heals an Officer's Servant

Jesus went to the city of Capernaum. When he entered the city, an army officer came to him and begged for help. The officer said, "Lord, my servant is very sick at home in bed. He can't move his body and has much pain."

Jesus said to the officer, "I will go and heal him."

The officer answered, "Lord, I am not good enough for you to come into my house. You need only to give the order, and my servant will be healed. I know this, because I understand authority. There are people who have authority over me, and I have soldiers under my authority. I tell one soldier, 'Go,' and he goes. I tell another soldier, 'Come,' and he comes. I say to my servant, 'Do this,' and my servant obeys me."

When Jesus heard this, he was amazed. He said to those who were with him, "The truth is, this man has more faith than anyone I have found, even in Israel. Many people will come from the east and from the west. These people will sit and eat with Abraham, Isaac, and Jacob in God's kingdom. And those who should have the kingdom will be thrown out. They will be thrown outside into the darkness, where people will cry and grind their teeth with pain."

Then Jesus said to the officer, "Go home. Your servant will be healed the way you believed he would." Right then his servant was healed.[86]

3.36 Jesus Brings a Woman's Son Back to Life

The next day Jesus and his followers went to a town called Nain. A big crowd was traveling with them. When Jesus came near the town gate, he saw some people carrying a dead body. It was the only son of a woman who was a widow. Walking with her were many other people from the town. When the Lord saw the woman, he felt very sorry for her and said, "Don't cry." He walked to the open coffin and touched it. The men who were carrying the coffin stopped. Jesus spoke to the dead son: "Young man, I tell you, get up!" Then the boy sat up and began to talk, and Jesus gave him back to his mother.

Everyone was filled with fear. They began praising God and said, "A great prophet is here with us!" and "God is taking care of his people."

This news about Jesus spread all over Judea and to all the other places around there.[87]

3.37 Jesus and John the Baptizer

John's followers told him about all these things. John called for two of his followers. He sent them to the Lord to ask, "Are you the one we heard was coming, or should we wait for someone else?"

So the men came to Jesus. They said, "John the Baptizer sent us to you with this question: 'Are you the one who is coming, or should we wait for someone else?'"

Right then Jesus healed many people of their sicknesses and diseases. He healed those who had evil spirits and made many who were blind able to see again. Then he said to John's followers, "Go tell John what you have seen and heard: The blind can see. The crippled can walk. People with leprosy are healed. The deaf can hear. The dead are brought back to life. And the Good News is being told to the poor. Great blessings belong to those who don't have a problem accepting me."

When John's followers left, Jesus began talking to the people about John: "What did you people go out into the desert to see? Someone who is weak, like a stem of grass blowing in the wind? Really, what did you expect to see? Someone dressed in fine clothes? Of course not. People who wear fancy clothes and live in luxury are all in kings' palaces. So what did you go out to see? A prophet? Yes, John is a prophet. But I tell you, he is more than that. This Scripture was written about him:

'Listen! I will send my messenger ahead of you.
   He will prepare the way for you.'

I tell you, no one ever born is greater than John. But even the least important person in God's kingdom is greater than John."

(When the people heard this, they all agreed that God's teaching was good. Even the tax collectors agreed. These were the people who were baptized by John. But the Pharisees and experts in the law refused to accept God's plan for themselves; they did not let John baptize them.)

"What shall I say about the people of this time? What can I compare them to? What are they like? They are like children sitting in the marketplace. One group of children calls to the other children and says,

'We played flute music for you,
   but you did not dance;
we sang a sad song,
   but you did not cry.'

John the Baptizer came and did not eat the usual food or drink wine. And you say, 'He has a demon inside him.' The Son of Man came eating and drinking. And you say, 'Look at him! He eats too much and drinks too much wine! He is a friend of tax collectors and other sinners!' But wisdom is shown to be right by those who accept it."[88]

3.38 Jesus Offers Rest to His People

Then Jesus said, "I praise you, Father, Lord of heaven and earth. I am thankful that you have hidden these things from those who are so wise and so smart. But you have shown them to people who are like little children. Yes, Father, you did this because it's what you really wanted to do.

"My Father has given me everything. No one knows the Son—only the Father knows the Son. And no one knows the Father—only the Son knows the Father. And the only people who will know about the Father are those the Son chooses to tell.

"Come to me all of you who are tired from the heavy burden you have been forced to carry. I will give you rest. Accept my teaching. Learn from me. I am gentle and humble in spirit. And you will be able to get some rest. Yes, the teaching that I ask you to accept is easy. The load I give you to carry is light."[89]

3.39 Jesus and a Sinful Woman

One of the Pharisees asked Jesus to eat with him. Jesus went into the Pharisee's house and took a place at the table.

There was a sinful woman in that town. She knew that Jesus was eating at the Pharisee's house. So the woman brought some expensive perfume in an alabaster jar. She stood at Jesus' feet, crying. Then she began to wash his feet with her tears. She dried his feet with her hair. She kissed his feet many times and rubbed them with the perfume.

When the Pharisee who asked Jesus to come to his house saw this, he thought to himself, "If this man were a prophet, he would know that the woman who is touching him is a sinner!"

In response, Jesus said to the Pharisee, "Simon, I have something to say to you."

Simon said, "Let me hear it, Teacher."

Jesus said, "There were two men. Both men owed money to the same banker. One man owed him 500 silver coins. The other man owed him 50 silver coins. The men had no money, so they could not pay their debt. But the banker told the men that they did not have to pay him. Which one of those two men will love him more?"

Simon answered, "I think it would be the one who owed him the most money."

Jesus said to him, "You are right." Then he turned to the woman and said to Simon, "Do you see this woman? When I came into your house, you gave me no water for my feet. But she washed my feet with her tears and dried my feet with her hair. You did not greet me with a kiss, but she has been kissing my feet since I came in. You did not honor me with oil for my head, but she rubbed my feet with her sweet-smelling oil. I tell you that her many sins are forgiven. This is clear, because she showed great love. People who are forgiven only a little will love only a little."

Then Jesus said to her, "Your sins are forgiven."

The people sitting at the table began to think to themselves, "Who does this man think he is? How can he forgive sins?"

Jesus said to the woman, "Because you believed, you are saved from your sins. Go in peace."[90]

3.40 Jesus in Galilee

The next day, Jesus traveled through some cities and small towns. Jesus told the people a message from God, the Good News about God's kingdom. The twelve apostles were with him. There were also some women with him. Jesus had healed these women of sicknesses and evil spirits. One of them was Mary, who was called Magdalene. Seven demons had come out of her. Also with these women were Joanna, the wife of Chuza (the manager of Herod's property), Suzanna, and many other women. These women used their own money to help Jesus and his apostles.[91]

3.41 Jesus' Power Is From God

Then some people brought a man to Jesus. This man was blind and could not talk, because he had a demon inside him. Jesus healed the man, and he could talk and see. All the people were amazed. They said, "Maybe this man is the Son of David!"

When the Pharisees heard this, they said, "This man uses the power of Satan to force demons out of people. Satan is the ruler of demons."

Jesus knew what the Pharisees were thinking. So he said to them, "Every kingdom that fights against itself will be destroyed. And every city or family that is divided against itself will not survive. So if Satan forces out his own demons, then he is fighting against himself, and his kingdom will not survive. You say that I use the power of Satan to force out demons. If that is true, then what power do your people use when they force out demons? So your own people will prove that you are wrong. But I use the power of God's Spirit to force out demons, and this shows that God's kingdom has come to you. Whoever wants to enter a strong man's house and steal his things must first tie him up.

Then they can steal the things from his house. Whoever is not with me is against me. And anyone who does not work with me is working against me.

"So I tell you, people can be forgiven for every sinful thing they do and for every bad thing they say against God. But anyone who speaks against the Holy Spirit will not be forgiven. You can even speak against the Son of Man and be forgiven. But anyone who speaks against the Holy Spirit will never be forgiven—not now or in the future.

"If you want good fruit, you must make the tree good. If your tree is not good, it will have bad fruit. A tree is known by the kind of fruit it produces. You snakes! You are so evil. How can you say anything good? What people say with their mouths comes from what fills their hearts. Those who are good have good things saved in their hearts. That's why they say good things. But those who are evil have hearts full of evil, and that's why they say things that are evil. I tell you that everyone will have to answer for all the careless things they have said. This will happen on the day of judgment. Your words will be used to judge you. What you have said will show whether you are right or whether you are guilty."92

3.42 Some People Doubt Jesus' Authority

Then some of the Pharisees and teachers of the law answered Jesus. They said, "Teacher, we want to see you do a miracle as a sign from God."

Jesus answered, "Evil and sinful people are the ones who want to see a miracle as a sign. But no miracle will be done to prove anything to them. The only sign will be the miracle that happened to the prophet Jonah. Jonah was in the stomach of the big fish for three days and three nights. In the same way, the Son of Man will be in the grave three days and three nights. On the judgment day, you people who live now will be compared with the people from Nineveh, and they will be witnesses who show how guilty you are. Why do I say this? Because when Jonah preached to those people, they changed their lives. And you are listening to someone greater than Jonah, but you refuse to change!

"On the judgment day, you people who live now will also be compared with the Queen of the South, and she will be a witness who shows how guilty you are. I say this because she traveled from far, far away to listen to Solomon's wise teaching. And I tell you that someone greater than Solomon is right here, but you won't listen!

"When an evil spirit comes out of a person, it travels through dry places looking for a place to rest, but it finds none. So it says, 'I will go back to the home I left.' When it comes back, it finds that home still empty. It is all neat and clean. Then the evil spirit goes out and brings seven other spirits more evil than itself. They all go and live there, and that person has even more trouble than before. It is the same way with the evil people who live today."[93]

3.43 Jesus' Followers Are His True Family

While Jesus was talking to the people, his mother and brothers stood outside. They wanted to talk to him. Someone told him, "Your mother and brothers are waiting for you outside. They want to talk to you."

Jesus answered, "Who is my mother? Who are my brothers?" Then he pointed to his followers and said, "See! These people are my mother and my brothers. My true brother and sister and mother is anyone who does what my Father in heaven wants."[94]

As Jesus was saying these things, a woman with the people there called out to him, "Blessings from God belong to the woman who gave birth to and fed you!"

But Jesus said, "The people who hear the teaching of God and obey it—they are the ones who have God's blessing."[95]

3.44 The Story About the Farmer Sowing Seed

That same day Jesus went out of the house and sat by the lake. A large crowd gathered around him. So he got into a boat and sat down. All the people stayed on the shore. Then Jesus used stories to teach them many things. He told them this story:

"A farmer went out to sow seed. While he was scattering the seed, some of it fell by the road. The birds came and ate all that seed. Other seed fell on rocky ground, where there was not enough dirt. It grew very fast there, because the soil was not deep. But when the sun rose, it burned the plants. The plants died because they did not have deep roots. Some other seed fell among thorny weeds. The weeds grew and stopped the good plants from growing. But some of the seed fell on good ground. There it grew and made grain. Some plants made 100 times more grain, some 60 times more, and some 30 times more. You people who hear me, listen!"

The followers came to Jesus and asked, "Why do you use these stories to teach the people?"

Jesus answered, "Only you can know the secret truths about God's kingdom. Those other people cannot know these secret truths. The people who have some understanding will be given more. And they will have even more than they need. But those who do not have much understanding will lose even the little understanding that they have. This is why I use these stories to teach the people: They see, but they don't really see. They hear, but they don't really hear or understand. So they show that what Isaiah said about them is true:

'You people will listen and listen,
  but you will not understand.
You will look and look,
  but you will not really see.
Yes, the minds of these people are now closed.
  They have ears, but they don't listen.
  They have eyes, but they refuse to see.
If their minds were not closed,
  they might see with their eyes;
  they might hear with their ears;
  they might understand with their minds.
Then they might turn back to me and be healed.'

But God has blessed you. You understand what you see with your eyes. And you understand what you hear with your ears. I can assure you, many prophets and godly people wanted to see what you now see. But they did not see it. And many prophets and godly people wanted to hear what you now hear. But they did not hear it.

"So listen to the meaning of that story about the farmer:

"What about the seed that fell by the path? That is like the people who hear the teaching about God's kingdom but do not understand it. The Evil One comes and takes away what was planted in their hearts.

"And what about the seed that fell on rocky ground? That is like the people who hear the teaching and quickly and gladly accept it. But they do not let the teaching go deep into their lives. They keep it only a short time. As soon as trouble or persecution comes because of the teaching they accepted, they give up.

"And what about the seed that fell among the thorny weeds? That is like the people who hear the teaching but let worries about this life and love for money stop it from growing. So it does not produce a crop in their lives.

"But what about the seed that fell on the good ground? That is like the people who hear the teaching and understand it. They grow and produce a good crop, sometimes 100 times more, sometimes 60 times more, and sometimes 30 times more."[96]

3.45 Use the Understanding You Have

Then Jesus said to them, "You don't take a lamp and hide it under a bowl or a bed, do you? Of course not. You put it on a lampstand. Everything that is hidden will be made clear. Every secret thing will be made known. You people who hear me, listen! Think carefully about what you are hearing. God will know how much to give you by how much you understand now. But he will give you more than you deserve. The people who have some understanding will receive more. But those who do not have much will lose even the small amount they have."[97]

3.46 Jesus Uses the Story About the Growing Seed

Then Jesus said, "God's kingdom is like a man who plants seed in the ground. The seed begins to grow. It grows night and day. It doesn't matter whether the man is sleeping or awake, the seed still grows. He doesn't know how it happens. Without any help the ground produces grain. First the plant grows, then the head, and then all the grain in the head. When the grain is ready, the man cuts it. This is the harvest time."[98]

3.47 The Story About the Wheat and Weeds

Then Jesus used another story to teach them. Jesus said, "God's kingdom is like a man who planted good seed in his field. That night, while everyone was asleep, the man's enemy came and planted weeds among the wheat and then left. Later, the wheat grew, and heads of grain grew on the plants. But at the same time the weeds also grew. Then the man's servants came to him and said, 'You planted good seed in your field. Where did the weeds come from?'

"The man answered, 'An enemy planted weeds.'

"The servants asked, 'Do you want us to go and pull up the weeds?'

"He answered, 'No, because when you pull up the weeds, you might also pull up the wheat. Let the weeds and the wheat grow together until the harvest time. At the harvest time I will tell the workers this: First, gather the weeds and tie them together to be burned. Then gather the wheat and bring it to my barn.'"[99]

3.48 The Stories About the Mustard Seed and the Yeast

Then Jesus told the people another story: "God's kingdom is like a mustard seed that a man plants in his field. It is the smallest of all seeds. But when it grows, it is the largest of all garden plants. It becomes a tree big enough for the birds to come and make nests in its branches."

Then Jesus told them another story: "God's kingdom is like yeast that a woman mixes into a big bowl of flour to make bread. The yeast makes all the dough rise."[100]

Jesus used many stories like these to teach the people. He taught them all they could understand. He always used stories to teach them. But when he was alone with his followers, Jesus explained everything to them.[101]

This was to make clear the full meaning of what the prophet said:

"I will speak using stories;
 I will tell things that have been secrets since the world was made."[102]

3.49 Jesus Explains the Story About the Weeds

Then Jesus left the people and went into the house. His followers came to him and said, "Explain to us the meaning of the story about the weeds in the field."

He answered, "The man who planted the good seed in the field is the Son of Man. The field is the world. The good seed are the people in God's kingdom. The weeds are the people who belong to the Evil One. And the enemy who planted the bad seed is the devil. The harvest is the end of time. And the workers who gather are God's angels.

"The weeds are pulled up and burned in the fire. It will be the same at the end of time. The Son of Man will send his angels, and they will find the people who cause sin and all those who do evil. The angels will take those people out of his kingdom. They will throw them into the place of fire. There the people will be crying and grinding their teeth with pain. Then the godly people will shine like the sun. They will be in the kingdom of their Father. You people who hear me, listen!"[103]

3.50 The Stories About the Treasure and the Pearl

"God's kingdom is like a treasure hidden in a field. One day a man found the treasure. He hid it again and was so happy that he went and sold everything he owned and bought the field.

"Also, God's kingdom is like a merchant looking for fine pearls. One day he found a very fine pearl. He went and sold everything he had to buy it."[104]

3.51 The Story About the Fishing Net

"Also, God's kingdom is like a net that was put into the lake. The net caught many different kinds of fish. It was full, so the fishermen pulled it to the shore. They sat down and put all the good fish in baskets. Then they threw away the bad fish. It will be the same at the end of time. The angels will come and separate the evil people from the godly people. They will throw the evil people into the place of fire. There the people will cry and grind their teeth with pain."

Then Jesus asked his followers, "Do you understand all these things?"

They said, "Yes, we understand."

Then Jesus said to the followers, "So every teacher of the law who has learned about God's kingdom has some new things to teach. He is like the owner of a house. He has new things and old things saved in that house. And he brings out the new with the old."

When Jesus finished teaching with these stories, he left there.[105]

3.52 Jesus Calms the Storm

That evening, Jesus said to his followers, "Come with me across the lake." So they left the crowd behind and went with Jesus in the boat he was already in. There were also other boats that went with them. A very bad wind came up on the lake. The waves were coming over the sides and into the boat, and it was almost full of water. Jesus was inside the boat, sleeping with his head on a pillow. The followers went and woke him. They said, "Teacher, don't you care about us? We are going to drown!"

Jesus stood up and gave a command to the wind and the water. He said, "Quiet! Be still!" Then the wind stopped, and the lake became calm.

He said to his followers, "Why are you afraid? Do you still have no faith?"

They were very afraid and asked each other, "What kind of man is this? Even the wind and the water obey him!"[106]

3.53 Jesus Frees a Man From Evil Spirits

Jesus and his followers sailed on across the lake. They sailed to the area where the Gerasene people live, across from Galilee. When Jesus got out of the boat, a man from that town came to him. This man had demons inside him. For a long time he had worn no clothes. He did not live in a house but in the caves where the dead are buried.[107]

No one could keep him tied up, even with chains. Many times people had put chains on his hands and feet, but he broke the chains. No one was strong enough to control him. Day and night he stayed around the burial caves and on the hills. He would scream and cut himself with rocks.

While Jesus was still far away, the man saw him. He ran to Jesus and bowed down before him. As Jesus was saying, "You evil spirit, come out of this man," the man shouted loudly, "What do you want with me, Jesus, Son of the Most High God? I beg you in God's name not to punish me!"

Then Jesus asked the man, "What is your name?"

The man answered, "My name is Legion, because there are many spirits inside me." The spirits inside the man begged Jesus again and again not to send them out of that area.

A large herd of pigs was eating on a hill near there. The evil spirits begged Jesus, "Send us to the pigs. Let us go into them." So Jesus allowed them to do this. The evil spirits left the man and went into the pigs. Then the herd of pigs ran down the hill and into the lake. They were all drowned. There were about 2000 pigs in that herd.

The men who had the work of caring for the pigs ran away. They ran to the town and to the farms and told everyone what happened. The people went out to see. They came to Jesus, and they saw the man who had the many evil spirits. He was sitting down and was wearing clothes. He was in his right mind again. When they saw this, they were afraid. Those who had seen what Jesus did told the others what happened to the man who had the demons living in him. And they also told about the pigs. Then the people began to beg Jesus to leave their area.

Jesus was preparing to leave in the boat. The man who was now free from the demons begged to go with him. But Jesus did not allow the man to go. He said, "Go home to your family and friends. Tell them about all that the Lord did for you. Tell them how the Lord was good to you."

So the man left and told the people in the Ten Towns about the great things Jesus did for him. Everyone was amazed.[108]

3.54 Jesus Gives Life to a Dead Girl and Heals a Sick Woman

Jesus went back to the other side of the lake in the boat. There, a large crowd of people gathered around him on the shore. A leader of the synagogue came. His name was Jairus. He saw Jesus and bowed down before him. He begged Jesus again and again, saying, "My little daughter is dying. Please come and lay your hands on her. Then she will be healed and will live."

So Jesus went with Jairus. Many people followed Jesus. They were pushing very close around him.

There among the people was a woman who had been bleeding for the past twelve years. She had suffered very much. Many doctors had tried to help her, and all the money she had was spent, but she was not improving. In fact, her sickness was getting worse.

The woman heard about Jesus, so she followed him with the other people and touched his coat. She thought, "If I can just touch his clothes, that will be enough to heal me." As soon as she touched his coat, her bleeding stopped. She felt that her body was healed from all the suffering. Jesus immediately felt power go out from him, so he stopped and turned around. "Who touched my clothes?" he asked.

The followers said to Jesus, "There are so many people pushing against you. But you ask, 'Who touched me?'"

But Jesus continued looking for the one who touched him. The woman knew that she was healed, so she came and bowed at Jesus' feet. She was shaking with fear. She told Jesus the whole story. He said to her, "Dear woman, you are made well because you believed. Go in peace. You will not suffer anymore."

While Jesus was still there speaking, some men came from the house of Jairus, the synagogue leader. They said, "Your daughter is dead. There is no need to bother the Teacher."

But Jesus did not care what the men said. He said to the synagogue leader, "Don't be afraid; just believe."

Jesus let only Peter, James, and John the brother of James go with him. They went to the synagogue leader's house, where Jesus saw many people crying loudly. There was a lot of confusion. He entered the house and said, "Why are you people crying and making so much noise? This child is not dead. She is only sleeping." But everyone laughed at him.

Jesus told the people to leave the house. Then he went into the room where the child was. He brought the child's father and mother and his three followers into the room with him. Then Jesus held the girl's hand and said to her, "*Talitha, koum!*" (This means "Little girl, I tell you to stand up!") The girl immediately stood up and began walking. (She was twelve years old.) The father and mother and the followers were amazed. Jesus gave the father and mother very strict orders not to tell people about this. Then he told them to give the girl some food to eat.[109]

3.55 Jesus Heals Two Blind Men

As Jesus was going away from there, two blind men followed him. They said loudly, "Show kindness to us, Son of David."

Jesus went inside, and the blind men went with him. He asked them, "Do you believe that I am able to make you see again?" They answered, "Yes, Lord, we believe."

Then Jesus touched their eyes and said, "You believe that I can make you see again, so it will happen." Then the men were able to see. Jesus gave them a strong warning. He said, "Don't tell anyone about this." But they left and spread the news about Jesus all around that area.

As these two men were leaving, some people brought another man to Jesus. This man could not talk because he had a demon inside him. Jesus forced the demon out, and the man was able to talk. The people were amazed and said, "We have never seen anything like this in Israel."

But the Pharisees said, "The ruler of demons is the one that gives him power to force demons out."[110]

3.56 Jesus Rejected in His Hometown

Jesus left and went back to his hometown. His followers went with him. On the Sabbath day Jesus taught in the synagogue, and many people heard him. They were amazed and said, "Where did this man get this teaching? How did he get such wisdom? Who gave it to him? And where did he get the power to do miracles? Isn't he just the carpenter we know—Mary's son, the brother of James, Joses, Judas, and Simon? And don't his sisters still live here in town?" So they had a problem accepting him.

Then Jesus said to them, "People everywhere give honor to a prophet, except in his own town, with his own people, or in his home." Jesus was not able to do any miracles there except the healing of some sick people by laying his hands on them. He was surprised that the people there had no faith.[111]

4 The Year of Opposition

4.1 Pray for Workers

Jesus traveled through all the towns and villages. He taught in their synagogues and told people the Good News about God's kingdom. He healed all kinds of diseases and sicknesses. Jesus saw the many people and felt sorry for them because they were worried and helpless—like sheep without a shepherd to lead them. Jesus said to his followers, "There is such a big harvest of people to bring in. But there are only a few workers to help harvest them. God owns the harvest. Ask him to send more workers to help gather his harvest."[112]

4.2 Jesus Sends Out the Twelve Apostles

Jesus called his twelve followers together. He gave them power over evil spirits and power to heal every kind of disease and sickness.[113]

Jesus sent the twelve men out with these instructions: "Don't go to the non-Jewish people. And don't go into any town where the Samaritans live. But go to the people of Israel. They are like sheep that are lost. When you go, tell them this: 'God's kingdom is coming soon.' Heal the sick. Bring the dead back to life. Heal the people who have leprosy. And force demons out of people. I give you these powers freely, so help others freely. Don't carry any money with you—gold or silver or copper. Don't carry a bag. Take only the clothes and sandals you are wearing. And don't take a walking stick. A worker should be given what he needs.

"When you enter a city or town, find some worthy person there and stay in his home until you leave. When you enter that home, say, 'Peace be with you.' If the people in that home welcome you, they are worthy of your peace. May they have the peace you wished for them. But if they don't welcome you, they are not worthy of your peace. Take back the peace you wished for them. And if the people in a home or a town refuse to welcome you or listen to you, then leave that place

The Year of Opposition

and shake the dust off your feet. I can assure you that on the judgment day it will be worse for that town than for the people of Sodom and Gomorrah.

"Listen! I am sending you, and you will be like sheep among wolves. So be smart like snakes. But also be like doves and don't hurt anyone. Be careful! There are people who will arrest you and take you to be judged. They will whip you in their synagogues. You will be taken to stand before governors and kings. People will do this to you because you follow me. You will tell about me to those kings and governors and to the non-Jewish people. When you are arrested, don't worry about what to say or how you should say it. At that time you will be given the words to say. It will not really be you speaking; the Spirit of your Father will be speaking through you.

"Brothers will turn against their own brothers and hand them over to be killed. Fathers will hand over their own children to be killed. Children will fight against their own parents and will have them killed. Everyone will hate you because you follow me. But the one who remains faithful to the end will be saved. When you are treated badly in one city, go to another city. I promise you that you will not finish going to all the cities of Israel before the Son of Man comes again.

"Students are not better than their teacher. Servants are not better than their master. Students should be happy to be treated the same as their teacher. And servants should be happy to be treated the same as their master. If those people call me 'the ruler of demons,' and I am the head of the family, then it is even more certain that they will insult you, the members of the family!

"So don't be afraid of those people. Everything that is hidden will be shown. Everything that is secret will be made known. I tell you all this secretly, but I want you to tell it publicly. Whatever I tell you privately, you should shout for everyone to hear.

"Don't be afraid of people. They can kill the body, but they cannot kill the soul. The only one you should fear is God, the one who can send the body and the soul to be destroyed in hell. When birds are sold, two small birds cost only a penny. But not even one of those little birds can die without your Father knowing it. God even knows how many hairs are on your head. So don't be afraid. You are worth more than a whole flock of birds.

"If you stand before others and are willing to say you believe in me, then I will tell my Father in heaven that you belong to me. But if you stand before others and say you do not believe in me, then I will tell my Father in heaven that you do not belong to me.

"Do not think that I have come to bring peace to the earth. I did not come to bring peace. I came to bring trouble. I have come to make this happen:

'A son will turn against his father.
A daughter will turn against her mother.
A daughter-in-law will turn against her mother-in-law.
Even members of your own family will be your enemies.'

"Those who love their father or mother more than they love me are not worthy of me. And those who love their son or daughter more than they love me are not worthy of me. Those who will not accept the cross that is given to them when they follow me are not worthy of me. Those who try to keep the life they have will lose it. But those who give up their life for me will find true life.

"Whoever accepts you also accepts me. And whoever accepts me accepts the one who sent me. Whoever accepts a prophet because he is a prophet will get the same reward a prophet gets. And whoever accepts a godly person just because that person is godly will get the same reward a godly person gets. Whoever helps one of these little ones because they are my followers will definitely get a reward, even if they only give them a cup of cold water."[114]

So the apostles went out. They traveled through all the towns.[115]

They talked to the people and told them to change their hearts and lives. They forced many demons out of people and put olive oil on many who were sick and healed them.[116]

When Jesus finished these instructions for his twelve followers, he left there. He went to the towns in Galilee to teach the people and tell them God's message.[117]

4.3 How John the Baptizer Was Killed

King Herod heard about Jesus, because Jesus was now famous. Some people said, "He is John the Baptizer. He must have risen from death, and that is why he can do these miracles."

Other people said, "He is Elijah."

The Year of Opposition

And others said, "He is a prophet. He is like the prophets who lived long ago."

Herod heard these things about Jesus. He said, "I killed John by cutting off his head. Now he has been raised from death![118] And that is why he can do these miracles."[119]

Herod himself had ordered his soldiers to arrest John and put him in prison. Herod did this to please his wife Herodias. She had been married to Herod's brother Philip, but then Herod married her. John told Herod, "It is not right for you to be married to your brother's wife." So Herodias hated John. She wanted him dead, but she was not able to persuade Herod to kill him. Herod was afraid to kill John, because he knew that he was a good and holy man. So he protected him. He liked listening to John, although what John said left him with so many questions.

Then the right time came for Herodias to cause John's death. It happened on Herod's birthday. Herod gave a dinner party for the most important government leaders, the commanders of his army, and the most important people in Galilee. The daughter of Herodias came to the party and danced. When she danced, Herod and the people eating with him were very pleased.

So King Herod said to the girl, "I will give you anything you want." He promised her, "Anything you ask for I will give to you—even half of my kingdom."

The girl went to her mother and asked, "What should I ask King Herod to give me?"

Her mother answered, "Ask for the head of John the Baptizer."

So right then the girl went back in to the king. She said to him, "Please give me the head of John the Baptizer. Bring it to me now on a plate."

King Herod was very sad, but he didn't want to break the promise he had made to her in front of his guests. So he sent a soldier to cut off John's head and bring it to him. The soldier went and cut off John's head in the prison. He brought the head back on a plate and gave it to the girl, and the girl gave it to her mother. John's followers heard about what happened, so they came and got John's body and put it in a tomb.[120]

Then they went and told Jesus what happened.[121]

4.4 Jesus Feeds More Than Five Thousand

The apostles Jesus had sent out came back to him. They gathered around him and told him about all they had done and taught. Jesus and his followers were in a very busy place. There were so many people that he and his followers did not even have time to eat. He said to them, "Come with me. We will go to a quiet place to be alone. There we will get some rest."

So Jesus and his followers went away alone. They went in a boat to a place where no one lived. But many people saw them leave and knew who they were. So people from every town ran to the place where they were going and got there before Jesus. As Jesus stepped out of the boat, he saw a large crowd waiting. He felt sorry for them, because they were like sheep without a shepherd to care for them. So he taught the people many things.

It was now very late in the day. Jesus' followers came to him and said, "No one lives around here, and it is already very late. So send the people away. They need to go to the farms and towns around here to buy some food to eat."

But Jesus answered, "You give them some food to eat."

They said to Jesus, "We can't buy enough bread to feed all these people. We would all have to work a month to earn enough to buy that much bread!"[122]

Philip answered, "We would all have to work a month to buy enough bread for each person here to have only a little piece!"

Another follower there was Andrew, the brother of Simon Peter. Andrew said, "Here is a boy with five loaves of barley bread and two little fish. But that is not enough for so many people."

Jesus said, "Tell everyone to sit down." This was a place with a lot of grass, and about 5000 men sat down there. Jesus took the loaves of bread and gave thanks for them. Then he gave them to the people who were waiting to eat. He did the same with the fish. He gave them as much as they wanted.

They all had plenty to eat. When they finished, Jesus said to his followers, "Gather the pieces of fish and bread that were not eaten. Don't waste anything." So they gathered up the pieces that were left. The people had started eating with only five loaves of barley bread. But the followers filled twelve large baskets with the pieces of food that were left.

The people saw this miraculous sign that Jesus did and said, "He must be the Prophet who is coming into the world."

Jesus knew that the people planned to come get him and make him their king.[123]

Then Jesus told the followers to get into the boat. He told them to go to the other side of the lake to Bethsaida. He said he would come later. He stayed there to tell everyone they could go home.[124]

After Jesus said goodbye to the people, he went up into the hills by himself to pray.[125]

4.5 Jesus Walks on the Water

It was late, and he was there alone. By this time the boat was already a long way from shore. Since the wind was blowing against it, the boat was having trouble because of the waves.

Between three and six o'clock in the morning, Jesus' followers were still in the boat. Jesus came to them. He was walking on the water. When they saw him walking on the water, it scared them. "It's a ghost!" they said, screaming in fear.

But Jesus quickly spoke to them. He said, "Don't worry! It's me! Don't be afraid."

Peter said, "Lord, if that is really you, tell me to come to you on the water."

Jesus said, "Come, Peter."

Then Peter left the boat and walked on the water to Jesus. But while Peter was walking on the water, he saw the wind and the waves. He was afraid and began sinking into the water. He shouted, "Lord, save me!"

Then Jesus caught Peter with his hand. He said, "Your faith is small. Why did you doubt?"

After Peter and Jesus were in the boat, the wind stopped. Then the followers in the boat worshiped Jesus and said, "You really are the Son of God."[126]

4.6 Jesus Heals Many Sick People

Jesus and his followers went across the lake and came to shore at Gennesaret. They tied the boat there. When they were out of the boat, the people there saw Jesus. They knew who he was, so they ran to tell others throughout that area. They brought sick people on mats to every place Jesus went. Jesus went into towns, cities, and farms around that area. And every place he went, the people brought sick people to the marketplaces. They begged him to let them touch any part of his coat. And all those who touched him were healed.[127]

4.7 Jesus, the Bread of Life

The next day came. Some people had stayed on the other side of the lake. They knew that Jesus did not go with his followers in the boat. They knew that the followers had left in the boat alone. And they knew it was the only boat that was there. But then some boats from Tiberias came and landed near the place where the people had eaten the day before. This was where they had eaten the bread after the Lord gave thanks. The people saw that Jesus and his followers were not there now. So they got into the boats and went to Capernaum to find Jesus.

The people found Jesus on the other side of the lake. They asked him, "Teacher, when did you come here?"

He answered, "Why are you looking for me? Is it because you saw miraculous signs? The truth is, you are looking for me because you ate the bread and were satisfied. But earthly food spoils and ruins. So don't work to get that kind of food. But work to get the food that stays good and gives you eternal life. The Son of Man will give you that food. He is the only one qualified by God the Father to give it to you."

The people asked Jesus, "What does God want us to do?"

Jesus answered, "The work God wants you to do is this: to believe in the one he sent."

So the people asked, "What miraculous sign will you do for us? If we can see you do a miracle, then we will believe you. What will you do? Our ancestors were given manna to eat in the desert. As the Scriptures say, 'He gave them bread from heaven to eat.'"

Jesus said, "I can assure you that Moses was not the one who gave your people bread from heaven. But my Father gives you the true bread from heaven. God's bread is the one who comes down from heaven and gives life to the world."

The people said, "Sir, from now on give us bread like that."

Then Jesus said, "I am the bread that gives life. No one who comes to me will ever be hungry. No one who believes in me will ever be thirsty. I told you before that you have seen me, and still you don't believe. The Father gives me my people. Every one of them will come to me. I will always accept them. I came down from heaven to do what God wants, not what I want. I must not lose anyone God has given me. But I must raise them up on the last day. This is what the one who sent me wants me to do. Everyone who sees the Son and believes in him has eternal life. I will raise them up on the last day. This is what my Father wants."

Some Jews began to complain about Jesus because he said, "I am the bread that comes down from heaven." They said, "This is Jesus. We know his father and mother. He is only Joseph's son. How can he say, 'I came down from heaven'?"

But Jesus said, "Stop complaining to each other. The Father is the one who sent me, and he is the one who brings people to me. I will raise them up on the last day. Anyone the Father does not bring to me cannot come to me. It is written in the prophets: 'God will teach them all.' People listen to the Father and learn from him. They are the ones who come to me. I don't mean that there is anyone who has seen the Father. The only one who has ever seen the Father is the one who came from God. He has seen the Father.

"I can assure you that anyone who believes has eternal life. I am the bread that gives life. Your ancestors ate the manna God gave them in the desert, but it didn't keep them from dying. Here is the bread that comes down from heaven. Whoever eats this bread will never die. I am the living bread that came down from heaven. Whoever eats this bread will live forever. This bread is my body. I will give my body so that the people in the world can have life."

Then the Jews began to argue among themselves. They said, "How can this man give us his body to eat?"

Jesus said, "Believe me when I say that you must eat the body of the Son of Man, and you must drink his blood. If you don't do this, you have no real life. Those who eat my body and drink my blood have eternal life. I will raise them up on the last day. My body is true food, and my blood is true drink. Those who eat my body and drink my blood live in me, and I live in them.

"The Father sent me. He lives, and I live because of him. So everyone who eats me will live because of me. I am not like the bread that your ancestors ate. They ate that bread, but they still died. I am the bread that came down from heaven. Whoever eats this bread will live forever."

Jesus said all this while he was teaching in the synagogue in the city of Capernaum.[128]

4.8 Many Followers Leave Jesus

When Jesus' followers heard this, many of them said, "This teaching is hard. Who can accept it?"

Jesus already knew that his followers were complaining about this. So he said, "Is this teaching a problem for you? Then what will you think when you see the Son of Man going up to where he came from? It is the Spirit that gives life. The body is of no value for that. But the things I have told you are from the Spirit, so they give life. But some of you don't believe." (Jesus knew the people who did not believe. He knew this from the beginning. And he knew the one who would hand him over to his enemies.) Jesus said, "That is why I said, 'Anyone the Father does not help to come to me cannot come.'"

After Jesus said these things, many of his followers left and stopped following him.

Jesus asked the twelve apostles, "Do you want to leave too?"

Simon Peter answered him, "Lord, where would we go? You have the words that give eternal life. We believe in you. We know that you are the Holy One from God."

Then Jesus answered, "I chose all twelve of you. But one of you is a devil." He was talking about Judas, the son of Simon Iscariot. Judas was one of the twelve apostles, but later he would hand Jesus over to his enemies.

After this, Jesus traveled around the country of Galilee. He did not want to travel in Judea, because the Jewish leaders there wanted to kill him.[129]

4.9 God's Law and Human Traditions

Some Pharisees and some teachers of the law came from Jerusalem and gathered around Jesus. They saw that some of his followers ate food with hands that were not clean, meaning that they did not wash their hands in a special way. The Pharisees and all the other Jews never eat before washing their hands in this special way. They do this to follow the traditions they have from their great leaders who lived long ago. And when these Jews buy something in the market, they never eat it until they wash it in a special way. They also follow other rules from their people who lived before them. They follow rules like the washing of cups, pitchers, and pots.

The Pharisees and teachers of the law said to Jesus, "Your followers don't follow the traditions we have from our great leaders who lived long ago. They eat their food with hands that are not clean. Why do they do this?"

Jesus answered, "You are all hypocrites. Isaiah was right when he wrote these words from God about you:

'These people honor me with their words,
  but I am not really important to them.
Their worship of me is worthless.
The things they teach are only human rules.'

You have stopped following God's commands, preferring instead the man-made rules you got from others."

Then he said, "You show great skill in avoiding the commands of God so that you can follow your own teachings! Moses said, 'You must respect your father and mother.' He also said, 'Whoever says anything bad to their father or mother must be killed.' But you teach that people can say to their father or mother, 'I have something I could use to help you, but I will not use it for you. I will give it to God.' You are telling people that they do not have to do anything for their father or mother. So you are teaching that it is not important to do what God said. You think it is more important to follow those traditions you have, which you pass on to others. And you do many things like that."

Jesus called the people to him again. He said, "Everyone should listen to me and understand what I am saying. There is nothing people can put in their mouth that will make them wrong. People are made wrong by what comes from inside them."[130]

Then the followers came to Jesus and asked, "Do you know that the Pharisees are upset about what you said?"

Jesus answered, "Every plant that my Father in heaven has not planted will be pulled up by the roots. Stay away from the Pharisees. They lead the people, but they are like blind men leading other blind men. And if a blind man leads another blind man, both of them will fall into a ditch."

Peter said, "Explain to us what you said earlier to the people."

Jesus said, "Do you still have trouble understanding? Surely you know that all the food that enters the mouth goes into the stomach. Then it goes out of the body. But the bad things people say with their mouth come from the way they think. And that's what can make people wrong. All these bad things begin in the mind: evil thoughts, murder, adultery, sexual sins, stealing, lying, and insulting people. These are the things that make people wrong. Eating without washing their hands will never make people unacceptable to God."

4.10 Jesus Helps a Canaanite Woman

Jesus went from there to the area of Tyre and Sidon. A Canaanite woman from that area came out and began shouting, "Lord, Son of David, please help me! My daughter has a demon inside her, and she is suffering very much."

But Jesus did not answer her. So the followers came to him and said, "Tell her to go away. She keeps crying out and will not leave us alone."

Jesus answered, "God sent me only to the lost people of Israel."

Then the woman came over to Jesus and bowed before him. She said, "Lord, help me!"

He answered her with this saying: "It is not right to take the children's bread and give it to the dogs."

The woman said, "Yes, Lord, but even the dogs eat the pieces of food that fall from their master's table."

Then Jesus answered, "Woman, you have great faith! You will get what you asked for." And right then the woman's daughter was healed.[131]

4.11 Jesus Heals a Deaf Man

Then Jesus left the area around Tyre and went through Sidon. On his way to Lake Galilee he went through the area of the Ten Towns.[132]

A large crowd of people came to him. They brought many other sick people and put them before him. There were people who could not walk, people who were blind, crippled, or deaf, and many others. Jesus healed them all.[133]

While he was there, some people brought a man to him who was deaf and could not talk clearly. The people begged Jesus to put his hand on the man to heal him.

Jesus led the man away from the people to be alone with him. He put his fingers in the man's ears. Then he spit on a finger and put it on the man's tongue. Jesus looked up to the sky and with a loud sigh he said, "*Ephphatha!*" (This means "Open!") As soon as Jesus did this, the man was able to hear. He was able to use his tongue, and he began to speak clearly.

Jesus told the people not to tell anyone about this. But the more he told them not to say anything, the more people they told.[134]

People were amazed when they saw that those who could not speak were now able to speak. Crippled people were made strong. Those who could not walk were now able to walk. The blind were able to see.[135]

They said, "Look at what he has done. It's all good. He makes deaf people able to hear and gives a new voice to people who could not talk."[136]

And they praised the God of Israel.[137]

4.12 Jesus Feeds More Than Four Thousand

Jesus called his followers to him and said, "I feel sorry for these people. They have been with me three days, and now they have nothing to eat. I don't want to send them away hungry. They might faint while going home."

The followers asked Jesus, "Where can we get enough bread to feed all these people? We are a long way from any town."

Jesus asked, "How many loaves of bread do you have?"

They answered, "We have seven loaves of bread and a few small fish."

Jesus told the people to sit on the ground. He took the seven loaves of bread and the fish. Then he gave thanks to God for the food. He broke the bread into pieces, which he gave to the followers, and they gave the food to the people. All the people ate until they were full. After this, the followers filled seven baskets with the pieces of food that were not eaten. There were about 4000 men there who ate. There were also some women and children. After they all ate, Jesus told the people they could go home. He got into the boat and went to the area of Magadan.[138]

4.13 Some People Doubt Jesus' Authority

The Pharisees and Sadducees came to Jesus. They wanted to test him. So they asked him to show them a miracle as a sign from God.

Jesus answered, "When you people see the sunset, you know what the weather will be. If the sky is red, you say we will have good weather. And in the morning, if the sky is dark and red, you say that it will be a rainy day. These are signs of the weather. You see these signs in the sky and know what they mean. In the same way, you see the things that are happening now. These are also signs, but you don't know their meaning. It is the evil and sinful people who want to see a miracle as a sign from God. But no miracle will be done to prove anything to them. The only sign will be the miracle that happened to Jonah." Then Jesus went away from there.[139]

4.14 Jesus' Followers Misunderstand Him

Jesus and his followers went across the lake. But the followers forgot to bring bread. Jesus said to the followers, "Be careful! Guard against the yeast of the Pharisees and the Sadducees."

The followers discussed the meaning of this. They said, "Did Jesus say this because we forgot to bring bread?"

Jesus knew that they were talking about this. So he asked them, "Why are you talking about not having bread? Your faith is small. Do you still not understand? Remember the five loaves of bread that fed the 5000 people and the many baskets you filled with the bread that was left? And remember the seven loaves of bread that fed the 4000 people and the many baskets you filled that time? So how could you think that I am concerned about bread? I am telling you to be careful and guard against the yeast of the Pharisees and the Sadducees."

Then the followers understood what Jesus meant. He was not telling them to guard against the yeast used in bread. He was telling them to guard against the teaching of the Pharisees and the Sadducees.[140]

4.15 Jesus Heals a Blind Man in Bethsaida

Jesus and his followers came to Bethsaida. Some people brought a blind man to him and begged him to touch the man. So Jesus held the blind man's hand and led him out of the village. Then he spit on the man's eyes. He laid his hands on him and asked, "Can you see now?"

The man looked up and said, "Yes, I see people. They look like trees walking around."

Again Jesus laid his hands on the man's eyes, and the man opened them wide. His eyes were healed, and he was able to see everything clearly. Jesus told him to go home. He said, "Don't go into the town."[141]

4.16 Peter Says Jesus Is the Messiah

Jesus went to the area of Caesarea Philippi. He said to his followers, "Who do people say I am?"

They answered, "Some people say you are John the Baptizer. Others say you are Elijah. And some say you are Jeremiah or one of the prophets."

Then Jesus said to his followers, "And who do you say I am?"

Simon Peter answered, "You are the Messiah, the Son of the living God."

Jesus answered, "You are blessed, Simon son of Jonah. No one taught you that. My Father in heaven showed you who I am. So I tell you, you are Peter. And I will build my church on this rock. The power of death will not be able to defeat my church. I will give you the keys to God's kingdom. When you speak judgment here on earth, that judgment will be God's judgment. When you promise forgiveness here on earth, that forgiveness will be God's forgiveness."

Then Jesus warned his followers not to tell anyone he was the Messiah.[142]

4.17 Jesus Says He Must Die

From that time Jesus began telling his followers that he must go to Jerusalem. He explained that the older Jewish leaders, the leading priests, and the teachers of the law would make him suffer many things. And he told his followers that he must be killed. Then, on the third day, he would be raised from death.

Peter took Jesus away from the other followers to talk to him alone. He began to criticize him. He said, "God save you from those sufferings, Lord! That will never happen to you!"

Then Jesus said to Peter, "Get away from me, Satan! You are not helping me! You don't care about the same things God does. You care only about things that people think are important."

Then Jesus said to his followers, "If any of you want to be my follower, you must stop thinking about yourself and what you want. You must be willing to carry the cross that is given to you for following me. Any of you who try to save the life you have will lose it. But you who give up your life for me will find true life. It is worth nothing for you to have the whole world if you yourself are lost. You could never pay enough to buy back your life.[143]

"Don't be ashamed of me and my teaching. If that happens, I will be ashamed of you when I come with my divine greatness and that of the Father and the holy angels.[144] And he will reward everyone for what they have done. Believe me when I say that there are some people standing here who will see the Son of Man coming with his kingdom before they die."[145]

4.18 Jesus Is Seen With Moses and Elijah

Six days later, Jesus took Peter, James, and John the brother of James and went up on a high mountain. They were all alone there[146] to pray. While Jesus was praying,[147] as these followers watched him, Jesus was changed. His face became bright like the sun, and his clothes became white as light.[148]

Then two men were there, talking with him. They were Moses and Elijah. They also looked bright and glorious. They were talking with Jesus about his death that would happen in Jerusalem. Peter and the others were asleep. But they woke up and saw the glory of Jesus. They also saw the two men who were standing with him. When Moses and Elijah were leaving, Peter said, "Master, it is good that we are here. We will put three tents here—one for you, one for Moses, and one for Elijah." (He did not know what he was saying.)[149]

While Peter was talking, a bright cloud came over them. A voice came from the cloud and said, "This is my Son, the one I love. I am very pleased with him. Obey him!"

The followers with Jesus heard this voice. They were very afraid, so they fell to the ground. But Jesus came to them and touched them. He said, "Stand up. Don't be afraid." The followers looked up, and they saw that Jesus was now alone.

As Jesus and the followers were coming down the mountain, he gave them this command: "Don't tell anyone about what you saw on the mountain. Wait until the Son of Man has been raised from death. Then you can tell people about what you saw."

The followers asked Jesus, "Why do the teachers of the law say that Elijah must come before the Messiah comes?"

Jesus answered, "They are right to say Elijah is coming. And it is true that Elijah will make all things the way they should be. But I tell you, Elijah has already come. People did not know who he was, and they treated him badly, doing whatever they wanted to do. It is the same with the Son of Man. Those same people will make the Son of Man suffer." Then the followers understood that when Jesus said Elijah, he was really talking about John the Baptizer.[150]

4.19 Jesus Frees a Boy From an Evil Spirit

Jesus and the followers went back to the people. A man came to Jesus and bowed before him. The man said, "Lord, be kind to my son. He suffers so much from the seizures he has. He often falls into the fire or into the water. I brought him to your followers, but they could not heal him."

Jesus answered, "You people today have no faith. Your lives are so wrong! How long must I stay with you? How long must I continue to be patient with you? Bring the boy here."[151]

So the followers brought the boy to Jesus. When the evil spirit saw Jesus, it attacked the boy. The boy fell down and rolled on the ground. He was foaming at the mouth.

Jesus asked the boy's father, "How long has this been happening to him?"

The father answered, "Since he was very young. The spirit often throws him into a fire or into water to kill him. If you can do anything, please have pity on us and help us."

Jesus said to the father, "Why did you say 'if you can'? All things are possible for the one who believes."

Immediately the father shouted, "I do believe. Help me to believe more!"

Jesus saw that all the people were running there to see what was happening. So he spoke to the evil spirit. He said, "You evil spirit that makes this boy deaf and stops him from talking—I command you to come out of him and never enter him again!"

The evil spirit screamed. It caused the boy to fall on the ground again, and then it came out. The boy looked as if he was dead. Many people said, "He is dead!" But Jesus took hold of his hand and helped him stand up.

Then Jesus went into the house. His followers were alone with him there. They said, "Why weren't we able to force that evil spirit out?"

Jesus answered, "That kind of spirit can be forced out only with prayer."[152]

4.20 Jesus Talks About His Death and Resurrection

Then Jesus and his followers left there and went through Galilee. Jesus did not want the people to know where they were. He wanted to teach his followers alone. He said to them, "The Son of Man will be handed over to the control of other men, who will kill him. After three days, he will rise from death." But the followers did not understand what he meant, and they were afraid to ask him.[153]

4.21 Jesus Teaches About Paying Taxes

Jesus and his followers went to Capernaum. There the men who collect the two-drachma Temple tax came to Peter and asked, "Does your teacher pay the Temple tax?"

Peter answered, "Yes, he does."

Peter went into the house where Jesus was. Before Peter could speak, Jesus said to him, "The kings on the earth get different kinds of taxes from people. But who are those who pay the taxes? Are they the king's children? Or do other people pay the taxes? What do you think?"

Peter answered, "The other people pay the taxes."

Jesus said, "Then the children of the king don't have to pay taxes. But we don't want to upset these tax collectors. So do this: Go to the lake and fish. After you catch the first fish, open its mouth. Inside its mouth you will find a four-drachma coin. Take that coin and give it to the tax collectors. That will pay the tax for you and me."[154]

4.22 Who Is the Greatest in God's Kingdom?

About that time the followers came to Jesus and asked, "Who is the greatest in God's kingdom?"

Jesus called a little child to come to him. He stood the child in front of the followers. Then he said, "The truth is, you must change your thinking and become like little children. If you don't do this, you will never enter God's kingdom. The greatest person in God's kingdom is the one who makes himself humble like this child.

"Whoever accepts a little child like this in my name is accepting me.[155]

Then John said, "Teacher, we saw a man using your name to force demons out of someone. He is not one of us. So we told him to stop, because he does not belong to our group."

Jesus said, "Don't stop him. Whoever uses my name to do powerful things will not soon say bad things about me. Whoever is not against us is with us. I can assure you that anyone who helps you by giving you a drink of water because you belong to the Messiah will definitely get a reward.[156]

"If one of these little children believes in me, and someone causes that child to sin, it will be very bad for that person. It would be better for them to have a millstone tied around their neck and be drowned in the deep sea. I feel sorry for the people in the world because of the things that make people sin. These things must happen, but it will be very bad for anyone who causes them to happen.

"If your hand or your foot makes you sin, cut it off and throw it away. It is better for you to lose part of your body and have eternal life than to have two hands and two feet and be thrown into the fire that burns forever. If your eye makes you sin, take it out and throw it away. It is better for you to have only one eye and have eternal life than to have two eyes and be thrown into the fire of hell.

"Be careful. Don't think these little children are not important. I tell you that these children have angels in heaven. And those angels are always with my Father in heaven.

"If a man has 100 sheep, but one of the sheep is lost, what will he do? He will leave the other 99 sheep on the hill and go look for the lost sheep. Right? And if he finds the lost sheep, he is happier about that one sheep than about the 99 sheep that were never lost. I can assure you, in the same way your Father in heaven does not want any of these little children to be lost."[157]

4.23 When Someone Hurts You

"If your brother or sister in God's family does something wrong, go and tell them what they did wrong. Do this when you are alone with them. If they listen to you, then you have helped them to be your brother or sister again. But if they refuse to listen, go to them again and take one or two people with you. Then there will be two or three people who will be able to tell all that happened. If they refuse to listen to them, then tell the church. And if they refuse to listen to the church, treat them as you would treat someone who does not know God or who is a tax collector.

"I can assure you that when you speak judgment here on earth, it will be God's judgment. And when you promise forgiveness here on earth, it will be God's forgiveness. To say it another way, if two of you on earth agree on anything you pray for, my Father in heaven will do what you ask. Yes, if two or three people are together believing in me, I am there with them."[158]

4.24 A Story About Forgiveness

Then Peter came to Jesus and asked, "Lord, when someone won't stop doing wrong to me, how many times must I forgive them? Seven times?"

Jesus answered, "I tell you, you must forgive them more than seven times. You must continue to forgive them even if they do wrong to you seventy-seven times."

"So God's kingdom is like a king who decided to collect the money his servants owed him. The king began to collect his money. One servant owed him several thousand pounds of silver. He was not able to pay the money to his master, the king. So the master ordered that he and everything he owned be sold, even his wife and children. The money would be used to pay the king what the servant owed.

"But the servant fell on his knees and begged, 'Be patient with me. I will pay you everything I owe.' The master felt sorry for him. So he told the servant he did not have to pay. He let him go free.

"Later, that same servant found another servant who owed him a hundred silver coins. He grabbed him around the neck and said, 'Pay me the money you owe me!'

"The other servant fell on his knees and begged, 'Be patient with me. I will pay you everything I owe.'

"But the first servant refused to be patient. He told the judge that the other servant owed him money, and that servant was put in jail until he could pay everything he owed. All the other servants saw what happened. They felt very sorry for the man. So they went and told their master everything that happened.

"Then the master called his servant in and said, 'You evil servant. You begged me to forgive your debt, and I said you did not have to pay anything! So you should have given that other man who serves with you the same mercy I gave you.' The master was very angry, so he put the servant in jail to be punished. And he had to stay in jail until he could pay everything he owed.

"This king did the same as my heavenly Father will do to you. You must forgive your brother or sister with all your heart, or my heavenly Father will not forgive you."[159]

4.25 Following Jesus

They were all traveling along the road. Someone said to Jesus, "I will follow you anywhere you go."

He answered, "The foxes have holes to live in. The birds have nests. But the Son of Man has no place where he can rest his head."

Jesus said to another man, "Follow me!"

But the man said, "Lord, let me go and bury my father first."

But Jesus said to him, "Let the people who are dead bury their own dead. You must go and tell about God's kingdom."

Another man said, "I will follow you, Lord, but first let me go and say goodbye to my family."

Jesus said, "Anyone who begins to plow a field but looks back is not prepared for God's kingdom."[160]

4.26 Jesus Goes to the Festival of Shelters

It was time for the Jewish Festival of Shelters. So his brothers said to him, "You should leave here and go to the festival in Judea. Then your followers there can see the miracles you do. If you want to be well-known, you must not hide what you do. So show yourself to the world. Let them see these things you do." Jesus' brothers said this because even they did not believe in him.

Jesus said to them, "The right time for me has not yet come, but any time is right for you to go. The world cannot hate you. But the world hates me, because I tell the people in the world that they do evil things. So you go to the festival. I will not go now, because the right time for me has not yet come." After Jesus said this, he stayed in Galilee.

So his brothers left to go to the festival. After they left, Jesus went too, but he did not let people see him. At the festival the Jewish leaders were looking for him. They said, "Where is that man?"

There was a large group of people there. Many of them were talking secretly to each other about Jesus. Some people said, "He is a good man." But others said, "No, he fools the people." But no one was brave enough to talk about him openly. They were afraid of the Jewish leaders.[161]

4.27 Jesus Teaches at the Festival

When the festival was about half finished, Jesus went to the Temple area and began to teach. The Jewish leaders were amazed and said, "How did this man learn so much? He never had the kind of teaching we had!"

Jesus answered, "What I teach is not my own. My teaching comes from the one who sent me. People who really want to do what God wants will know that my teaching comes from God. They will know that this teaching is not my own. If I taught my own ideas, I would just be trying to get honor for myself. But if I am trying to bring honor to the one who sent me, I can be trusted. Anyone doing that is not going to lie. Moses gave you the law, right? But you don't obey that law. If you do, then why are you trying to kill me?"

The people answered, "A demon is making you crazy! We are not trying to kill you."

Jesus said to them, "I did one miracle on a Sabbath day, and you were all surprised. But you obey the law Moses gave you about circumcision—and sometimes you do it on a Sabbath day. (Really, Moses is not the one who gave you circumcision. It came from our ancestors who lived before Moses.) Yes, you often circumcise baby boys on a Sabbath day. This shows that someone can be circumcised on a Sabbath day to obey the Law of Moses. So why are you angry with me for healing a person's whole body on the Sabbath day? Stop judging by the way things look. Be fair and judge by what is really right."[162]

4.28 The People Wonder if Jesus Is the Messiah

Then some of the people who lived in Jerusalem said, "This is the man they are trying to kill. But he is teaching where everyone can see and hear him. And no one is trying to stop him from teaching. Maybe the leaders have decided that he really is the Messiah. But when the real Messiah comes, no one will know where he comes from. And we know where this man's home is."

Jesus was still teaching in the Temple area when he said loudly, "Do you really know me and where I am from? I am here, but not by my own decision. I was sent by one who is very real. But you don't know him. I know him because I am from him. He is the one who sent me."

When Jesus said this, the people tried to grab him. But no one was able even to touch him, because the right time for him had not yet come. But many of the people believed in Jesus. They said, "We are waiting for the Messiah to come. When he comes, will he do more miraculous signs than this man has done?"

The Pharisees heard what the people were saying about Jesus. So the leading priests and the Pharisees sent some Temple police to arrest him. Then Jesus said, "I will be with you a little while longer. Then I will go back to the one who sent me. You will look for me, but you will not find me. And you cannot come where I am."

These Jews said to each other, "Where will this man go that we cannot find him? Will he go to the Greek cities where our people live? Will he teach the Greek people there? He says, 'You will look for me, but you will not find me.' He also says, 'You cannot come where I am.' What does this mean?"

The last day of the festival came. It was the most important day. On that day Jesus stood up and said loudly, "Whoever is thirsty may come to me and drink. If anyone believes in me, rivers of living water will flow out from their heart. That is what the Scriptures say." Jesus was talking about the Spirit. The Spirit had not yet been given to people, because Jesus had not yet been raised to glory. But later, those who believed in Jesus would receive the Spirit.

When the people heard the things that Jesus said, some of them said, "This man really is the Prophet."

Other people said, "He is the Messiah."

And others said, "The Messiah will not come from Galilee. The Scriptures say that he will come from the family of David. And they say that he will come from Bethlehem, the town where David lived." So the people did not agree with each other about Jesus. Some of the people wanted to arrest him. But no one tried to do it.[163]

4.29 Some Jewish Leaders Refuse to Believe

The Temple police went back to the leading priests and the Pharisees. The priests and the Pharisees asked, "Why didn't you bring Jesus?"

The Temple police answered, "We have never heard anyone say such amazing things!"

The Pharisees answered, "So he has fooled you too! You don't see any of the leaders or any of us Pharisees believing in him, do you? But those people out there know nothing about the law. They are under God's curse!"

But Nicodemus was there in that group. He was the one who had gone to see Jesus before. He said, "Our law will not let us judge anyone without first hearing them and finding out what they have done."

The Jewish leaders answered, "You must be from Galilee too! Study the Scriptures. You will find nothing about a prophet coming from Galilee."[164]

4.30 A Woman Caught in Adultery

Then they all left and went home.

Jesus went to the Mount of Olives. Early in the morning he went back to the Temple area. The people all came to him, and he sat and taught them.

The teachers of the law and the Pharisees brought a woman they had caught in bed with a man who was not her husband. They forced her to stand in front of the people. They said to Jesus, "Teacher, this woman was caught in the act of adultery. The Law of Moses commands us to stone to death any such woman. What do you say we should do?"

They were saying this to trick Jesus. They wanted to catch him saying something wrong so that they could have a charge against him. But Jesus stooped down and started writing on the ground with his finger. The Jewish leaders continued to ask him their question. So he stood up and said, "Anyone here who has never sinned should throw the first stone at her." Then Jesus stooped down again and wrote on the ground.

When they heard this, they began to leave one by one. The older men left first, and then the others. Jesus was left alone with the woman standing there in front of him. He looked up again and said to her,

"Where did they all go? Did no one judge you guilty?"

She answered, "No one, sir."

Then Jesus said, "I don't judge you either. You can go now, but don't sin again."[165]

4.31 Jesus Is the Light of the World

Later, Jesus talked to the people again. He said, "I am the light of the world. Whoever follows me will never live in darkness. They will have the light that gives life."

But the Pharisees said to Jesus, "When you talk about yourself, you are the only one to say that these things are true. So we cannot accept what you say."

Jesus answered, "Yes, I am saying these things about myself. But people can believe what I say, because I know where I came from. And I know where I am going. But you don't know where I came from or where I am going. You judge me the way people judge other people. I don't judge anyone. But if I judge, my judging is true, because when I judge I am not alone. The Father who sent me is with me. Your own law says that when two witnesses say the same thing, you must accept what they say. I am one of the witnesses who speaks about myself. And the Father who sent me is my other witness."

The people asked, "Where is your father?"

Jesus answered, "You don't know me or my Father. But if you knew me, you would know my Father too." Jesus said these things while he was teaching in the Temple area, near the room where the Temple offerings were kept. But no one arrested him, because the right time for him had not yet come.

Again, Jesus said to the people, "I will leave you. You will look for me, but you will die in your sin. You cannot come where I am going."

So the Jewish leaders asked themselves, "Will he kill himself? Is that why he said, 'You cannot come where I am going'?"

But Jesus said to them, "You people are from here below, but I am from above. You belong to this world, but I don't belong to this world. I told you that you would die in your sins. Yes, if you don't believe that I AM, you will die in your sins."

They asked, "Then who are you?"

Jesus answered, "I am what I have told you from the beginning. I have much more I could say to judge you. But I tell people only what I have heard from the one who sent me, and he speaks the truth."

They did not understand who he was talking about. He was telling them about the Father. So he said to them, "You will lift up the Son of Man. Then you will know that I AM. You will know that whatever I do is not by my own authority. You will know that I say only what the Father has taught me. The one who sent me is with me. I always do what pleases him. So he has not left me alone." While he was saying these things, many people believed in him.[166]

4.32 The Children of Abraham

So Jesus said to the Jews who believed in him, "If you continue to accept and obey my teaching, you are really my followers. You will know the truth, and the truth will make you free."

They answered, "We are Abraham's descendants. And we have never been slaves. So why do you say that we will be free?"

Jesus said, "The truth is, everyone who sins is a slave—a slave to sin. A slave does not stay with a family forever. But a son belongs to the family forever. So if the Son makes you free, you are really free. I know you are Abraham's descendants. But you want to kill me, because you don't want to accept my teaching. I am telling you what my Father has shown me. But you do what your father has told you."

They said, "Our father is Abraham."

Jesus said, "If you were really Abraham's descendants, you would do what Abraham did. I am someone who has told you the truth I heard from God. But you are trying to kill me. Abraham did nothing like that. So you are doing what your own father did."

But they said, "We are not like children who never knew who their father was. God is our Father. He is the only Father we have."[167]

4.33 The Children of the Devil

Jesus said to them, "If God were really your Father, you would love me. I came from God, and now I am here. I did not come by my own authority. God sent me. You don't understand the things I say, because you cannot accept my teaching. Your father is the devil. You belong to him. You want to do what he wants. He was a murderer from the beginning. He was always against the truth. There is no truth in him. He is like the lies he tells. Yes, the devil is a liar. He is the father of lies.

"I am telling you the truth, and that's why you don't believe me. Can any of you prove that I am guilty of sin? If I tell the truth, why don't you believe me? Whoever belongs to God accepts what he says. But you don't accept what God says, because you don't belong to God."[168]

4.34 Jesus Talks About Himself and Abraham

The Jews there answered, "We say you are a Samaritan. We say a demon is making you crazy! Are we not right when we say this?"

Jesus answered, "I have no demon in me. I give honor to my Father, but you give no honor to me. I am not trying to get honor for myself. There is one who wants this honor for me. He is the judge. I promise you, whoever continues to obey my teaching will never die."

The Jews said to Jesus, "Now we know that you have a demon in you! Even Abraham and the prophets died. But you say, 'Whoever obeys my teaching will never die.' Do you think you are greater than our father Abraham? He died, and so did the prophets. Who do you think you are?"

Jesus answered, "If I give honor to myself, that honor is worth nothing. The one who gives me honor is my Father. And you say that he is your God. But you don't really know him. I know him. If I said I did not know him, I would be a liar like you. But I do know him, and I obey what he says. Your father Abraham was very happy that he would see the day when I came. He saw that day and was happy."

The Jews said to Jesus, "What? How can you say you have seen Abraham? You are not even 50 years old!"

Jesus answered, "The fact is, before Abraham was born, I AM." When he said this, they picked up stones to throw at him. But Jesus hid, and then he left the Temple area.[169]

4.35 Jesus Heals a Man Born Blind

While Jesus was walking, he saw a man who had been blind since the time he was born. Jesus' followers asked him, "Teacher, why was this man born blind? Whose sin made it happen? Was it his own sin or that of his parents?"

Jesus answered, "It was not any sin of this man or his parents that caused him to be blind. He was born blind so that he could be used to show what great things God can do. While it is daytime, we must continue doing the work of the one who sent me. The night is coming, and no one can work at night. While I am in the world, I am the light of the world."

After Jesus said this, he spit on the dirt, made some mud and put it on the man's eyes. Jesus told him, "Go and wash in Siloam pool." (Siloam means "Sent.") So the man went to the pool, washed and came back. He was now able to see.

His neighbors and some others who had seen him begging said, "Look! Is this the same man who always sits and begs?"

Some people said, "Yes! He is the one." But others said, "No, he can't be the same man. He only looks like him."

So the man himself said, "I am that same man."

They asked, "What happened? How did you get your sight?"

He answered, "The man they call Jesus made some mud and put it on my eyes. Then he told me to go to Siloam and wash. So I went there and washed. And then I could see."

They asked him, "Where is this man?"

He answered, "I don't know."[170]

4.36 Some Religious Leaders Have Questions

Then the people brought the man to the Pharisees. The day Jesus had made mud and healed the man's eyes was a Sabbath day. So the Pharisees asked the man, "How did you get your sight?"

He answered, "He put mud on my eyes. I washed, and now I can see."

Some of the Pharisees said, "That man does not obey the law about the Sabbath day. So he is not from God."

Others said, "But someone who is a sinner cannot do these miraculous signs." So they could not agree with each other.

They asked the man again, "Since it was your eyes he healed, what do you say about him?"

He answered, "He is a prophet."

The Jewish leaders still did not believe that this really happened to the man—that he was blind and was now healed. But later they sent for his parents. They asked them, "Is this your son? You say he was born blind. So how can he see?"

His parents answered, "We know that this man is our son. And we know that he was born blind. But we don't know why he can see now. We don't know who healed his eyes. Ask him. He is old enough to answer for himself." They said this because they were afraid of the Jewish leaders. The leaders had already decided that they would punish anyone who said Jesus was the Messiah. They would stop them from coming to the synagogue. That is why his parents said, "He is old enough. Ask him."

So the Jewish leaders called the man who had been blind. They told him to come in again. They said, "You should honor God by telling the truth. We know that this man is a sinner."

The man answered, "I don't know if he is a sinner. But I do know this: I was blind, and now I can see."

They asked, "What did he do to you? How did he heal your eyes?"

He answered, "I have already told you that. But you would not listen to me. Why do you want to hear it again? Do you want to be his followers too?"

At this they shouted insults at him and said, "You are his follower, not us! We are followers of Moses. We know that God spoke to Moses. But we don't even know where this man comes from!"

The man answered, "This is really strange! You don't know where he comes from, but he healed my eyes. We all know that God does not listen to sinners, but he will listen to anyone who worships and obeys him. This is the first time we have ever heard of anyone healing the eyes of someone born blind. This man must be from God. If he were not from God, he could not do anything like this."

The Jewish leaders answered, "You were born full of sin! Are you trying to teach us?" And they told the man to get out of the synagogue and to stay out.[171]

4.37 *Spiritual Blindness*

When Jesus heard that they had forced the man to leave, he found him and asked him, "Do you believe in the Son of Man?"

The man said, "Tell me who he is, sir, so I can believe in him."

Jesus said to him, "You have already seen him. The Son of Man is the one talking with you now."

The man answered, "Yes, I believe, Lord!" Then he bowed and worshiped Jesus.

Jesus said, "I came into this world so that the world could be judged. I came so that people who are blind could see. And I came so that people who think they see would become blind."

Some of the Pharisees were near Jesus. They heard him say this. They asked, "What? Are you saying that we are blind too?"

Jesus said, "If you were really blind, you would not be guilty of sin. But you say that you see, so you are still guilty."[172]

4.38 The Shepherd and His Sheep

Jesus said, "It is certainly true that when a man enters the sheep pen, he should use the gate. If he climbs in some other way, he is a robber. He is trying to steal the sheep. But the man who takes care of the sheep enters through the gate. He is the shepherd. The man who guards the gate opens the gate for the shepherd. And the sheep listen to the voice of the shepherd. He calls his own sheep, using their names, and he leads them out. He brings all of his sheep out. Then he goes ahead of them and leads them. The sheep follow him, because they know his voice. But sheep will never follow someone they don't know. They will run away from him, because they don't know his voice."

Jesus told the people this story, but they did not understand what it meant.

So Jesus said again, "I assure you, I am the gate for the sheep. All those who came before me were thieves and robbers. The sheep did not listen to them. I am the gate. Whoever enters through me will be saved. They will be able to come in and go out. They will find everything they need. A thief comes to steal, kill, and destroy. But I came to give life—life that is full and good.

"I am the good shepherd, and the good shepherd gives his life for the sheep. The worker who is paid to keep the sheep is different from the shepherd. The paid worker does not own the sheep. So when he sees a wolf coming, he runs away and leaves the sheep alone. Then the wolf attacks the sheep and scatters them. The man runs away because he is only a paid worker. He does not really care for the sheep.

"I am the shepherd who cares for the sheep. I know my sheep just as the Father knows me. And my sheep know me just as I know the Father. I give my life for these sheep. I have other sheep too. They are not in this flock here. I must lead them also. They will listen to my voice. In the future there will be one flock and one shepherd. The Father loves me because I give my life. I give my life so that I can get it back again. No one takes my life away from me. I give my own life freely. I have the right to give my life, and I have the right to get it back again. This is what the Father told me."

Again the Jews were divided over what Jesus was saying. Many of them said, "A demon has come into him and made him crazy. Why listen to him?"

But others said, "These aren't the words of someone controlled by a demon. A demon cannot heal the eyes of a blind man."[173]

4.39 Jesus Sends Out Seventy-two of His Followers

After this, the Lord chose 72 more followers. He sent them out in groups of two. He sent them ahead of him into every town and place where he planned to go. He said to them, "There is such a big harvest of people to bring in. But there are only a few workers to help harvest them. God owns the harvest. Ask him to send more workers to help bring in his harvest.

"You can go now. But listen! I am sending you, and you will be like sheep among wolves. Don't carry any money, a bag, or sandals. Don't stop to talk with people on the road. Before you go into a house, say, 'Peace be with this home.' If the people living there love peace, your blessing of peace will stay with them. But if not, your blessing of peace will come back to you. Stay in the peace-loving house. Eat and drink what the people there give you. A worker should be given his pay. Don't leave that house to stay in another house.

"If you go into a town and the people welcome you, eat the food they give you. Heal the sick people who live there, and tell them, 'God's kingdom is coming to you soon!'

"But if you go into a town, and the people don't welcome you, then go out into the streets of that town and say, 'Even the dirt from your town that sticks to our feet we wipe off against you. But remember that God's kingdom is coming soon.' I tell you, on the judgment day it will be worse for the people of that town than for the people of Sodom.

"It will be bad for you, Chorazin! It will be bad for you, Bethsaida! I did many miracles in you. If those same miracles had happened in Tyre and Sidon, then the people in those cities would have changed their lives and stopped sinning a long time ago. They would have worn sackcloth and sat in ashes to show that they were sorry for their sins. But on the judgment day it will be worse for you than for Tyre and Sidon. And you, Capernaum, will you be lifted up to heaven? No, you will be thrown down to the place of death!

"When anyone listens to you my followers, they are really listening to me. But when anyone refuses to accept you, they are really refusing to accept me. And when anyone refuses to accept me, they are refusing to accept the one who sent me."

When the 72 followers came back from their trip, they were very happy. They said, "Lord, even the demons obeyed us when we used your name!"

Jesus said to them, "I saw Satan falling like lightning from the sky. He is the enemy, but know that I have given you more power than he has. I have given you power to crush his snakes and scorpions under your feet. Nothing will hurt you. Yes, even the spirits obey you. And you can be happy, not because you have this power, but because your names are written in heaven."

Then the Holy Spirit made Jesus feel very happy. Jesus said, "I praise you, Father, Lord of heaven and earth. I am thankful that you have hidden these things from those who are so wise and so smart. But you have shown them to people who are like little children. Yes, Father, you did this because it's what you really wanted to do.

"My Father has given me all things. No one knows who the Son is—only the Father knows. And only the Son knows who the Father is. The only people who will know about the Father are those the Son chooses to tell."

Then Jesus turned to his followers. They were there alone with him. He said, "It is a great blessing for you to see what you now see! I tell you, many prophets and kings wanted to see what you now see, but they could not. And they wanted to hear what you now hear, but they could not."[174]

4.40 The Most Important Commandment, the Story About the Good Samaritan

Then an expert in the law stood up to test Jesus. He said, "Teacher, what must I do to get eternal life?"

Jesus said to him, "What is written in the law? What do you understand from it?"

The man answered, "'Love the Lord your God with all your heart, all your soul, all your strength, and all your mind.' Also, 'Love your neighbor the same as you love yourself.'"

Jesus said, "Your answer is right. Do this and you will have eternal life."

But the man wanted to show that the way he was living was right. So he said to Jesus, "But who is my neighbor?"

To answer this question, Jesus said, "A man was going down the road from Jerusalem to Jericho. Some robbers surrounded him, tore off his clothes, and beat him. Then they left him lying there on the ground almost dead.

"It happened that a Jewish priest was going down that road. When he saw the man, he did not stop to help him. He walked away. Next, a Levite came near. He saw the hurt man, but he went around him. He would not stop to help him either. He just walked away.

"Then a Samaritan man traveled down that road. He came to the place where the hurt man was lying. He saw the man and felt very sorry for him. The Samaritan went to him and poured olive oil and wine on his wounds. Then he covered the man's wounds with cloth. The Samaritan had a donkey. He put the hurt man on his donkey, and he took him to an inn. There he cared for him. The next day, the Samaritan took out two silver coins and gave them to the man who worked at the inn. He said, 'Take care of this hurt man. If you spend more money on him, I will pay it back to you when I come again.'"

Then Jesus said, "Which one of these three men do you think was really a neighbor to the man who was hurt by the robbers?"

The teacher of the law answered, "The one who helped him."

Jesus said, "Then you go and do the same."[175]

4.41 Martha and Mary

While Jesus and his followers were traveling, he went into a town, and a woman named Martha let him stay at her house. She had a sister named Mary. Mary was sitting at Jesus' feet and listening to him teach. But her sister Martha was busy doing all the work that had to be done. Martha went in and said, "Lord, don't you care that my sister has left me to do all the work by myself? Tell her to help me!"

But the Lord answered her, "Martha, Martha, you are getting worried and upset about too many things. Only one thing is important. Mary has made the right choice, and it will never be taken away from her."[176]

4.42 Jesus Teaches About Prayer

One time Jesus was out praying, and when he finished, one of his followers said to him, "John taught his followers how to pray. Lord, teach us how to pray too."

Jesus said to the followers, "This is how you should pray:

'Father, we pray that your name will always be kept holy.
We pray that your kingdom will come.
Give us the food we need for each day.
Forgive our sins,
   just as we forgive everyone who has done wrong to us.
And don't let us be tempted.'"

Then Jesus said to them, "Suppose one of you went to your friend's house very late at night and said to him, 'A friend of mine has come into town to visit me. But I have nothing for him to eat. Please give me three loaves of bread.' Your friend inside the house answers, 'Go away! Don't bother me! The door is already locked. My children and I are in bed. I cannot get up and give you the bread now.' I tell you, maybe friendship is not enough to make him get up to give you the bread. But he will surely get up to give you what you need if you continue to ask. So I tell you, continue to ask, and God will give to you. Continue to search, and you will find. Continue to knock, and the door will open for you. Yes, whoever continues to ask will receive. Whoever continues to look will find. And whoever continues to knock will have the door opened for them. Do any of you have a son? What would you do if your son asked you for a fish? Would any father give him a snake? Or, if he asked for an egg, would you give him a scorpion? Of course not! Even you who are bad know how to give good things to your children. So surely your heavenly Father knows how to give the Holy Spirit to the people who ask him."[177]

4.43 Jesus Criticizes the Religious Leaders

After Jesus had finished speaking, a Pharisee asked Jesus to eat with him. So he went and took a place at the table. But the Pharisee was surprised when he saw that Jesus did not wash his hands first before the meal. The Lord said to him, "The washing you Pharisees do is like cleaning only the outside of a cup or a dish. But what is inside you?

You want only to cheat and hurt people. You are foolish! The same one who made what is outside also made what is inside. So pay attention to what is inside. Give to the people who need help. Then you will be fully clean.

"But it will be bad for you Pharisees! You give God a tenth of the food you get, even your mint, your rue, and every other little plant in your garden. But you forget to be fair to others and to love God. These are the things you should do. And you should also continue to do those other things.

"It will be bad for you Pharisees because you love to have the most important seats in the synagogues. And you love for people to show respect to you in the marketplaces. It will be bad for you, because you are like hidden graves. People walk on them without knowing it."

One of the experts in the law said to Jesus, "Teacher, when you say these things about the Pharisees, you are criticizing our group too."

Jesus answered, "It will be bad for you, you experts in the law! You make strict rules that are very hard for people to obey. You try to force others to obey your rules. But you yourselves don't even try to follow any of those rules. It will be bad for you, because you build tombs for the prophets. But these are the same prophets your ancestors killed! And now you show all people that you agree with what your ancestors did. They killed the prophets, and you build tombs for the prophets! This is why God in his wisdom said, 'I will send prophets and apostles to them. Some of my prophets and apostles will be killed by evil men. Others will be treated badly.'

"So you people who live now will be punished for the deaths of all the prophets who were killed since the beginning of the world. You will be punished for the killing of Abel. And you will be punished for the killing of Zechariah, who was killed between the altar and the Temple. Yes, I tell you that you people will be punished for them all.

"It will be bad for you, you experts in the law! You have taken away the key to learning about God. You yourselves would not learn, and you stopped others from learning too."

When Jesus went out, the teachers of the law and the Pharisees began to give him much trouble. They tried to make him answer questions about many things. They were trying to find a way to catch Jesus saying something wrong.[178]

4.44 Warning and Encouragement

Many thousands of people came together. There were so many people that they were stepping on each other. Before Jesus spoke to the people, he said to his followers, "Be careful of the yeast of the Pharisees. I mean that they are hypocrites. Everything that is hidden will be shown, and everything that is secret will be made known. What you say in the dark will be told in the light. And what you whisper in a private room will be shouted from the top of the house."

Then Jesus said to the people, "I tell you, my friends, don't be afraid of people. They can kill the body, but after that they can do nothing more to hurt you. I will show you the one to fear. You should fear God, who has the power to kill you and also to throw you into hell. Yes, he is the one you should fear.

"When birds are sold, five small birds cost only two pennies. But God does not forget any of them. Yes, God even knows how many hairs you have on your head. Don't be afraid. You are worth much more than many birds.

"I tell you, if you stand before others and are willing to say you believe in me, then I will say that you belong to me. I will say this in the presence of God's angels. But if you stand before others and say you do not believe in me, then I will say that you do not belong to me. I will say this in the presence of God's angels.

"Whoever says something against the Son of Man can be forgiven. But whoever speaks against the Holy Spirit will not be forgiven.

"When men bring you into the synagogues before the leaders and other important men, don't worry about what you will say. The Holy Spirit will teach you at that time what you should say."[179]

4.45 The Story About a Rich Fool

One of the men in the crowd said to Jesus, "Teacher, our father just died and left some things for us. Tell my brother to share them with me."

But Jesus said to him, "Who said I should be your judge or decide how to divide your father's things between you two?" Then Jesus said to them, "Be careful and guard against all kinds of greed. People do not get life from the many things they own."

Then Jesus used this story: "There was a rich man who had some land. His land grew a very good crop of food. He thought to himself,

'What will I do? I have no place to keep all my crops.'

"Then he said, 'I know what I will do. I will tear down my barns and build bigger barns! I will put all my wheat and good things together in my new barns. Then I can say to myself, I have many good things stored. I have saved enough for many years. Rest, eat, drink, and enjoy life!'

"But God said to that man, 'Foolish man! Tonight you will die. So what about the things you prepared for yourself? Who will get those things now?'

"This is how it will be for anyone who saves things only for himself. To God that person is not rich."[180]

4.46 Following Jesus May Bring You Trouble

Jesus continued speaking: "I came to bring fire to the world. I wish it were already burning! There is a kind of baptism that I must suffer through. I feel very troubled until it is finished. Do you think I came to give peace to the world? No, I came to divide the world! From now on, a family of five will be divided, three against two, and two against three.

> A father and son will be divided:
>   The son will turn against his father.
>   The father will turn against his son.
> A mother and her daughter will be divided:
>   The daughter will turn against her mother.
>   The mother will turn against her daughter.
> A mother-in-law and her daughter-in-law will be divided:
>   The daughter-in-law will turn against her mother-in-law.
>   The mother-in-law will turn against her daughter-in-law."[181]

4.47 Change Your Hearts

Some people there with Jesus at that time told him about what had happened to some worshipers from Galilee. Pilate had them killed. Their blood was mixed with the blood of the animals they had brought for sacrificing. Jesus answered, "Do you think this happened to those people because they were more sinful than all other people from Galilee? No, they were not. But if you don't decide now to change your lives, you will all be destroyed like those people! And what about those

18 people who died when the tower of Siloam fell on them? Do you think they were more sinful than everyone else in Jerusalem? They were not. But I tell you if you don't decide now to change your lives, you will all be destroyed too!"

Jesus told this story: "A man had a fig tree. He planted it in his garden. He came looking for some fruit on it, but he found none. He had a servant who took care of his garden. So he said to his servant, 'I have been looking for fruit on this tree for three years, but I never find any. Cut it down! Why should it waste the ground?' But the servant answered, 'Master, let the tree have one more year to produce fruit. Let me dig up the dirt around it and fertilize it. Maybe the tree will have fruit on it next year. If it still does not produce, then you can cut it down.'"[182]

4.48 Jesus Heals a Woman on the Sabbath

Jesus taught in one of the synagogues on the Sabbath day. A woman was there who had a spirit inside her. It had made the woman crippled for 18 years. Her back was always bent; she could not stand up straight. When Jesus saw her, he called to her, "Woman, you have been made free from your sickness!" He laid his hands on her, and immediately she was able to stand up straight. She began praising God.

The synagogue leader was angry because Jesus healed on the Sabbath day. He said to the people, "There are six days for work. So come to be healed on one of those days. Don't come for healing on the Sabbath day."

The Lord answered, "You people are hypocrites! All of you untie your work animals and lead them to drink water every day—even on the Sabbath day. This woman that I healed is a true descendant of Abraham. But Satan has held her for 18 years. Surely it is not wrong for her to be made free from her sickness on a Sabbath day!" When Jesus said this, all those who were criticizing him felt ashamed of themselves. And all the people were happy for the wonderful things he was doing.[183]

4.49 The Jewish Leaders Against Jesus

It was winter, and the time came for the Festival of Dedication at Jerusalem. Jesus was in the Temple area at Solomon's Porch. The Jewish leaders gathered around him. They said, "How long will you make us wonder about you? If you are the Messiah, then tell us clearly."

Jesus answered, "I told you already, but you did not believe. I do miracles in my Father's name. These miracles show who I am. But you do not believe, because you are not my sheep. My sheep listen to my voice. I know them, and they follow me. I give my sheep eternal life. They will never die, and no one can take them out of my hand. My Father is the one who gave them to me, and he is greater than all. No one can steal my sheep out of his hand. The Father and I are one."

Again the Jews there picked up stones to kill Jesus. But he said to them, "The many wonderful things you have seen me do are from the Father. Which of these good things are you killing me for?"

They answered, "We are not killing you for any good thing you did. But you say things that insult God. You are only a man, but you say you are the same as God! That is why we are trying to kill you!"

Jesus answered, "It is written in your law that God said, 'I said you are gods.' This Scripture called those people gods—the people who received God's message. And Scripture is always true. So why do you accuse me of insulting God for saying, 'I am God's Son'? I am the one God chose and sent into the world. If I don't do what my Father does, then don't believe what I say. But if I do what my Father does, you should believe in what I do. You might not believe in me, but you should believe in the things I do. Then you will know and understand that the Father is in me and I am in the Father."

They tried to get Jesus again, but he escaped from them.

Then he went back across the Jordan River to the place where John began his work of baptizing people. Jesus stayed there, and many people came to him. They said, "John never did any miraculous signs, but everything John said about this man is true." And many people there believed in Jesus.[184]

4.50 The Narrow Door

Jesus was teaching in every town and village. He continued to travel toward Jerusalem. Someone said to him, "Lord, how many people will be saved? Only a few?"

Jesus said, "The door to heaven is narrow. Try hard to enter it. Many people will want to enter there, but they will not be able to go in. If a man locks the door of his house, you can stand outside and knock on the door, but he won't open it. You can say, 'Sir, open the door for us.' But he will answer, 'I don't know you. Where did you come from?' Then you will say, 'We ate and drank with you. You taught in the streets of our town.' Then he will say to you, 'I don't know you. Where did you come from? Get away from me! You are all people who do wrong!'

"You will see Abraham, Isaac, Jacob, and all the prophets in God's kingdom. But you will be left outside. There you will cry and grind your teeth with pain. People will come from the east, west, north, and south. They will sit down at the table in God's kingdom. People who have the lowest place in life now will have the highest place in God's kingdom. And people who have the highest place now will have the lowest place in God's kingdom."[185]

4.51 Jesus Will Die in Jerusalem

Just then some Pharisees came to Jesus and said, "Go away from here and hide. Herod wants to kill you!"

Jesus said to them, "Go tell that fox, 'Today and tomorrow I am forcing demons out of people and finishing my work of healing. Then, the next day, the work will be finished.' After that, I must go, because all prophets should die in Jerusalem.

"Jerusalem, Jerusalem! You kill the prophets. You stone to death the people God has sent to you. How many times I wanted to help your people. I wanted to gather them together as a hen gathers her chicks under her wings. But you did not let me. Now your home will be left completely empty. I tell you, you will not see me again until that time when you will say, 'Welcome! God bless the one who comes in the name of the Lord.'"[186]

4.52 Jesus at a Pharisee's Home

On a Sabbath day, Jesus went to the home of a leading Pharisee to eat with him. The people there were all watching him very closely. A man with a bad disease was there in front of him. Jesus said to the Pharisees and experts in the law, "Is it right or wrong to heal on the Sabbath day?" But they would not answer his question. So he took the man and healed him. Then he sent the man away. Jesus said to the Pharisees and teachers of the law, "If your son or work animal falls into a well on the Sabbath day, you know you would pull him out immediately." The Pharisees and teachers of the law could say nothing against what he said.

Then Jesus noticed that some of the guests were choosing the best places to sit. So he told this story: "When someone invites you to a wedding, don't sit in the most important seat. They may have invited someone more important than you. And if you are sitting in the most important seat, they will come to you and say, 'Give this man your seat!' Then you will have to move down to the last place and be embarrassed.

"So when someone invites you, go sit in the seat that is not important. Then they will come to you and say, 'Friend, move up here to this better place!' What an honor this will be for you in front of all the other guests. Everyone who makes themselves important will be made humble. But everyone who makes themselves humble will be made important."

Then Jesus said to the Pharisee who had invited him, "When you give a lunch or a dinner, don't invite only your friends, brothers, relatives, and rich neighbors. At another time they will pay you back by inviting you to eat with them. Instead, when you give a feast, invite the poor, the crippled, and the blind. Then you will have great blessings, because these people cannot pay you back. They have nothing. But God will reward you at the time when all godly people rise from death."[187]

4.53 The Story About People Invited to the Dinner

One of the men sitting at the table with Jesus heard these things. The man said to him, "It will be a great blessing for anyone to eat a meal in God's kingdom!"

Jesus said to him, "A man gave a big dinner. He invited many people. When it was time to eat, he sent his servant to tell the guests, 'Come. The food is ready.' But all the guests said they could not come. Each one made an excuse. The first one said, 'I have just bought a field, so I must go look at it. Please excuse me.' Another man said, 'I have just bought five pairs of work animals; I must go and try them out. Please excuse me.' A third man said, 'I just got married; I can't come.'

"So the servant returned and told his master what happened. The master was angry. He said, 'Hurry! Go into the streets and alleys of the town. Bring me the poor, the crippled, the blind, and the lame.'

"Later, the servant said to him, 'Master, I did what you told me to do, but we still have places for more people.' The master said to the servant, 'Go out to the highways and country roads. Tell the people there to come. I want my house to be full! None of those people I invited first will get to eat any of this food.'"[188]

4.54 Decide if You Can Follow Me

Many people were traveling with Jesus. He said to them, "If you come to me but will not leave your family, you cannot be my follower. You must love me more than your father, mother, wife, children, brothers, and sisters—even more than your own life! Whoever will not carry the cross that is given to them when they follow me cannot be my follower.

"If you wanted to build a building, you would first sit down and decide how much it would cost. You must see if you have enough money to finish the job. If you don't do that, you might begin the work, but you would not be able to finish. And if you could not finish it, everyone would laugh at you. They would say, 'This man began to build, but he was not able to finish.'

"If a king is going to fight against another king, first he will sit down and plan. If he has only 10,000 men, he will try to decide if he is able to defeat the other king who has 20,000 men. If he thinks he cannot defeat the other king, he will send some men to ask for peace while that king's army is still far away.

"It is the same for each of you. You must leave everything you have to follow me. If not, you cannot be my follower.

"Salt is a good thing. But if the salt loses its salty taste, you can't make it salty again. It is worth nothing. You can't even use it as dirt or dung. People just throw it away.

"You people who hear me, listen!"[189]

4.55 The Story About the Lost Sheep

Many tax collectors and sinners came to listen to Jesus. Then the Pharisees and the teachers of the law began to complain, "Look, this man welcomes sinners and even eats with them!"

Then Jesus told them this story: "Suppose one of you has 100 sheep, but one of them gets lost. What will you do? You will leave the other 99 sheep there in the field and go out and look for the lost sheep. You will continue to search for it until you find it. And when you find it, you will be very happy. You will carry it home, go to your friends and neighbors and say to them, 'Be happy with me because I found my lost sheep!' In the same way, I tell you, heaven is a happy place when one sinner decides to change. There is more joy for that one sinner than for 99 good people who don't need to change."[190]

4.56 The Story About the Lost Coin

"Suppose a woman has ten silver coins, but she loses one of them. She will take a light and clean the house. She will look carefully for the coin until she finds it. And when she finds it, she will call her friends and neighbors and say to them, 'Be happy with me because I have found the coin that I lost!' In the same way, it's a happy time for the angels of God when one sinner decides to change."[191]

4.57 The Story About the Lost Son

Then Jesus said, "There was a man who had two sons. The younger son said to his father, 'Give me now the part of your property that I am supposed to receive someday.' So the father divided his wealth between his two sons.

"A few days later the younger son gathered up all that he had and left. He traveled far away to another country, and there he wasted his money living like a fool. After he spent everything he had, there was a terrible famine throughout the country. He was hungry and needed money. So he went and got a job with one of the people who lived there. The man sent him into the fields to feed pigs. He was so hungry that he wanted to eat the food the pigs were eating. But no one gave him anything.

"The son realized that he had been very foolish. He thought, 'All my father's hired workers have plenty of food. But here I am, almost dead because I have nothing to eat. I will leave and go to my father. I will say to him: Father, I have sinned against God and have done wrong to you. I am no longer worthy to be called your son. But let me be like one of your hired workers.' So he left and went to his father.

"While the son was still a long way off, his father saw him coming and felt sorry for him. So he ran to him and hugged and kissed him. The son said, 'Father, I have sinned against God and have done wrong to you. I am no longer worthy to be called your son.'

"But the father said to his servants, 'Hurry! Bring the best clothes and put them on him. Also, put a ring on his finger and good sandals on his feet. And bring our best calf and kill it so that we can celebrate with plenty to eat. My son was dead, but now he is alive again! He was lost, but now he is found!' So they began to have a party.

"The older son had been out in the field. When he came near the house, he heard the sound of music and dancing. So he called to one of the servant boys and asked, 'What does all this mean?' The boy said, 'Your brother has come back, and your father killed the best calf to eat. He is happy because he has his son back safe and sound.'

"The older son was angry and would not go in to the party. So his father went out and begged him to come in. But he said to his father, 'Look, for all these years I have worked like a slave for you. I have always done what you told me to do, and you never gave me even a young goat for a party with my friends. But then this son of yours comes home after wasting your money on prostitutes, and you kill the best calf for him!'

"His father said to him, 'Oh, my son, you are always with me, and everything I have is yours. But this was a day to be happy and celebrate. Your brother was dead, but now he is alive. He was lost, but now he is found.'"[192]

4.58 The Story About the Dishonest Manager

Jesus said to his followers, "Once there was a rich man. He hired a manager to take care of his business. Later, he learned that his manager was cheating him. So he called the manager in and said to him, 'I have heard bad things about you. Give me a report of what you have done with my money. You can't be my manager anymore.'

"So, the manager thought to himself, 'What will I do? My master is taking my job away from me. I am not strong enough to dig ditches. I am too proud to beg. I know what I will do! I will do something to make friends, so that when I lose my job, they will welcome me into their homes.'

"So the manager called in each person who owed the master some money. He asked the first one, 'How much do you owe my master?' He answered, 'I owe him 100 jars of olive oil.' The manager said to him, 'Here is your bill. Hurry! Sit down and make the bill less. Write 50 jars.'

"Then the manager asked another one, 'How much do you owe my master?' He answered, 'I owe him 100 measures of wheat.' Then the manager said to him, 'Here is your bill; you can make it less. Write 80 measures.'

"Later, the master told the dishonest manager that he had done a smart thing. Yes, worldly people are smarter in their business with each other than spiritual people are.

"I tell you, use the worldly things you have now to make 'friends' for later. Then, when those things are gone, you will be welcomed into a home that lasts forever. Whoever can be trusted with small things can also be trusted with big things. Whoever is dishonest in little things will be dishonest in big things too. If you cannot be trusted with worldly riches, you will not be trusted with the true riches. And if you cannot be trusted with the things that belong to someone else, you will not be given anything of your own.

"You cannot serve two masters at the same time. You will hate one master and love the other. Or you will be loyal to one and not care about the other. You cannot serve God and Money at the same time."

The Pharisees were listening to all these things. They criticized Jesus because they all loved money. Jesus said to them, "You make yourselves look good in front of people. But God knows what is really in your hearts. What people think is important is worth nothing to God."[193]

4.59 The Rich Man and the Poor Man

Jesus said, "There was a rich man who always dressed in the finest clothes. He was so rich that he was able to enjoy all the best things every day. There was also a very poor man named Lazarus. Lazarus' body was covered with sores. He was often put by the rich man's gate. Lazarus wanted only to eat the scraps of food left on the floor under the rich man's table. And the dogs came and licked his sores.

"Later, Lazarus died. The angels took him and placed him in the arms of Abraham. The rich man also died and was buried. He was sent to the place of death and was in great pain. He saw Abraham far away with Lazarus in his arms. He called, 'Father Abraham, have mercy on me! Send Lazarus to me so that he can dip his finger in water and cool my tongue. I am suffering in this fire!'

"But Abraham said, 'My child, remember when you lived? You had all the good things in life. But Lazarus had nothing but problems. Now he is comforted here, and you are suffering. Also, there is a big pit between you and us. No one can cross over to help you, and no one can come here from there.'

"The rich man said, 'Then please, father Abraham, send Lazarus to my father's house on earth. I have five brothers. He could warn my brothers so that they will not come to this place of pain.'

"But Abraham said, 'They have the Law of Moses and the writings of the prophets to read; let them learn from that.'

"The rich man said, 'No, father Abraham! But if someone came to them from the dead, then they would decide to change their lives.'

"But Abraham said to him, 'If your brothers won't listen to Moses and the prophets, they won't listen to someone who comes back from the dead.'"[194]

4.60 Forgiveness, Faith, and Duty

Jesus said to his followers, "Things will surely happen that will make people sin. But it will be very bad for anyone who makes this happen. It will be very bad for anyone who makes one of these little children sin. It would be better for them to have a millstone tied around their neck and be drowned in the sea. So be careful!

"If your brother or sister in God's family does something wrong, warn them. If they are sorry for what they did, forgive them. Even if they do something wrong to you seven times in one day, but they say they are sorry each time, you should forgive them."

The apostles said to the Lord, "Give us more faith!"

The Lord said, "If your faith is as big as a mustard seed, you can say to this mulberry tree, 'Dig yourself up and plant yourself in the ocean!' And the tree will obey you.

"Suppose one of you has a servant who has been working in the field, plowing or caring for the sheep. When he comes in from work, what would you say to him? Would you say, 'Come in, sit down and eat'? Of course not! You would say to your servant, 'Prepare something for me to eat. Then get ready and serve me. When I finish eating and drinking, then you can eat.' The servant should not get any special thanks for doing his job. He is only doing what his master told him to do. It is the same with you. When you finish doing all that you are told to do, you should say, 'We are not worthy of any special thanks. We have only done the work we should do.'"[195]

4.61 The Death of Lazarus

There was a man named Lazarus who was sick. He lived in the town of Bethany, where Mary and her sister Martha lived. (Mary is the same woman who put perfume on the Lord and wiped his feet with her hair.) Mary's brother was Lazarus, the man who was now sick. So Mary and Martha sent someone to tell Jesus, "Lord, your dear friend Lazarus is sick."

When Jesus heard this he said, "The end of this sickness will not be death. No, this sickness is for the glory of God. This has happened to bring glory to the Son of God." Jesus loved Martha and her sister and Lazarus. So when he heard that Lazarus was sick, he stayed where he was two more days and then said to his followers, "We should go back to Judea."

They answered, "But Teacher, those Jews there tried to stone you to death. That was only a short time ago. Now you want to go back there?"

Jesus answered, "There are twelve hours of light in the day. Whoever walks in the day will not stumble and fall because they can see with the light from the sun. But whoever walks at night will stumble because there is no light."

Then Jesus said, "Our friend Lazarus is now sleeping, but I am going there to wake him."

The followers answered, "But, Lord, if he can sleep, he will get well." They thought Jesus meant that Lazarus was literally sleeping, but he really meant that Lazarus was dead.

So then Jesus said plainly, "Lazarus is dead. And I am glad I was not there. I am happy for you because now you will believe in me. We will go to him now."

Then Thomas, the one called "Twin," said to the other followers, "We will go too. We will die there with Jesus."[196]

4.62 Jesus Comforts the Sisters of Lazarus

Jesus arrived in Bethany and found that Lazarus had already been dead and in the tomb for four days. Bethany was about two miles from Jerusalem. Many Jews had come to see Martha and Mary. They came to comfort them about their brother Lazarus.

When Martha heard that Jesus was coming, she went out to greet him. But Mary stayed home. Martha said to Jesus, "Lord, if you had been here, my brother would not have died. But I know that even now God will give you anything you ask."

Jesus said, "Your brother will rise and be alive again."

Martha answered, "I know that he will rise to live again at the time of the resurrection on the last day."

Jesus said to her, "I am the resurrection. I am life. Everyone who believes in me will have life, even if they die. And everyone who lives and believes in me will never really die. Martha, do you believe this?"

Martha answered, "Yes, Lord. I believe that you are the Messiah, the Son of God. You are the one who was coming to the world."

After Martha said these things, she went back to her sister Mary. She talked to Mary alone and said, "The Teacher is here. He is asking for you." When Mary heard this, she stood up and went quickly to Jesus. He had not yet come into the village. He was still at the place where Martha met him. The Jews who were in the house comforting Mary saw her get up and leave quickly. They thought she was going to the tomb to cry there. So they followed her. Mary went to the place where Jesus was. When she saw him, she bowed at his feet and said, "Lord, if you had been here, my brother would not have died."

When Jesus saw Mary crying and the people with her crying too, he was very upset and deeply troubled. He asked, "Where did you put him?"

They said, "Lord, come and see."

Jesus cried.

And the Jews said, "Look! He loved Lazarus very much!"

But some of them said, "Jesus healed the eyes of the blind man. Why didn't he help Lazarus and stop him from dying?"[197]

4.63 Jesus Raises Lazarus From Death

Again feeling very upset, Jesus came to the tomb. It was a cave with a large stone covering the entrance. He said, "Move the stone away."

Martha said, "But, Lord, it has been four days since Lazarus died. There will be a bad smell." Martha was the sister of the dead man.

Then Jesus said to her, "Remember what I told you? I said that if you believed, you would see God's divine greatness."

So they moved the stone away from the entrance. Then Jesus looked up and said, "Father, I thank you that you heard me. I know that you always hear me. But I said these things because of the people here around me. I want them to believe that you sent me." After Jesus said this he called in a loud voice, "Lazarus, come out!" The dead man came out. His hands and feet were wrapped with pieces of cloth. He had a handkerchief covering his face.

Jesus said to the people, "Take off the cloth and let him go."[198]

4.64 Religious Leaders Plan to Kill Jesus

There were many Jews who came to visit Mary. When they saw what Jesus did, many of them believed in him. But some of them went to the Pharisees and told them what Jesus did. Then the leading priests and Pharisees called a meeting of the high council. They said, "What should we do? This man is doing many miraculous signs. If we let him continue doing these things, everyone will believe in him. Then the Romans will come and take away our Temple and our nation."

One of the men there was Caiaphas. He was the high priest that year. He said, "You people know nothing! It is better for one man to die for the people than for the whole nation to be destroyed. But you don't realize this."

Caiaphas did not think of this himself. As that year's high priest, he was really prophesying that Jesus would die for the Jewish people. Yes, he would die for the Jewish people. But he would also die for God's other children scattered all over the world. He would die to bring them all together and make them one people.

That day the Jewish leaders began planning to kill Jesus. So Jesus stopped traveling around openly among the Jews. He went away to a town called Ephraim in an area near the desert. He stayed there with his followers.[199]

4.65 Jesus Heals Ten Men with Leprosy

Jesus was traveling to Jerusalem. He went from Galilee to Samaria. He came into a small town, and ten men met him there. They did not come close to him, because they all had leprosy. But the men shouted, "Jesus! Master! Please help us!"

When Jesus saw the men, he said, "Go and show yourselves to the priests."

While the ten men were going to the priests, they were healed. When one of them saw that he was healed, he went back to Jesus. He praised God loudly. He bowed down at Jesus' feet and thanked him. (He was a Samaritan.) Jesus said, "Ten men were healed; where are the other nine? This man is not even one of our people. Is he the only one who came back to give praise to God?" Then Jesus said to the man, "Stand up! You can go. You were healed because you believed."[200]

4.66 The Coming of God's Kingdom

Some of the Pharisees asked Jesus, "When will God's kingdom come?"

Jesus answered, "God's kingdom is coming, but not in a way that you can see it. People will not say, 'Look, God's kingdom is here!' or 'There it is!' No, God's kingdom is here with you."

Then Jesus said to his followers, "The time will come when you will want very much to see one of the days of the Son of Man, but you will not be able to. People will say to you, 'Look, there it is!' or 'Look, here it is!' Stay where you are; don't go away and search.

"When the Son of Man comes again, you will know it. On that day he will shine like lightning flashes across the sky. But first, the Son of Man must suffer many things. The people of today will refuse to accept him.

"When the Son of Man comes again, it will be the same as it was when Noah lived. People were eating, drinking, and getting married even on the day when Noah entered the boat. Then the flood came and killed them all.

"It will be the same as during the time of Lot, when God destroyed Sodom. Those people were eating, drinking, buying, selling, planting, and building houses for themselves. They were doing these things even on the day when Lot left town. Then fire and sulfur rained down from the sky and killed them all. This is exactly how it will be when the Son of Man comes again.

"On that day if a man is on his roof, he will not have time to go inside and get his things. If a man is in the field, he cannot go back home. Remember what happened to Lot's wife!

"Whoever tries to keep the life they have will lose it. But whoever gives up their life will save it. That night there may be two people sleeping in one room. One will be taken and the other will be left. There may be two women working together. One will be taken and the other will be left."

The followers asked Jesus, "Where will this be, Lord?"

Jesus answered, "It's like looking for a dead body—you will find it where the vultures are gathering above."[201]

4.67 The Story of the Widow Who Would Not Give Up

Then Jesus taught the followers that they should always pray and never lose hope. He used this story to teach them: "Once there was a judge in a town. He did not care about God. He also did not care what people thought about him. In that same town there was a woman whose husband had died. She came many times to this judge and said, 'There is a man who is doing bad things to me. Give me my rights!' But the judge did not want to help the woman. After a long time, the judge thought to himself, 'I don't care about God. And I don't care about what people think. But this woman is bothering me. If I give her what she wants, then she will leave me alone. But if I don't give her what she wants, she will bother me until I am sick.'"

The Lord said, "Listen, there is meaning in what the bad judge said. God's people shout to him night and day, and he will always give them what is right. He will not be slow to answer them. I tell you, God will help his people quickly. But when the Son of Man comes again, will he find people on earth who believe in him?"[202]

4.68 The Story About the Pharisee and the Tax Collector

There were some people who thought they were very good and looked down on everyone else. Jesus used this story to teach them: "One time there was a Pharisee and a tax collector. One day they both went to the Temple to pray. The Pharisee stood alone, away from the tax collector. When the Pharisee prayed, he said, 'O God, I thank you that I am not as bad as other people. I am not like men who steal, cheat, or commit adultery. I thank you that I am better than this tax collector. I fast twice a week, and I give a tenth of everything I get!'

"The tax collector stood alone too. But when he prayed, he would not even look up to heaven. He felt very humble before God. He said, 'O God, have mercy on me. I am a sinner!' I tell you, when this man finished his prayer and went home, he was right with God. But the Pharisee, who felt that he was better than others, was not right with God. People who make themselves important will be made humble. But those who make themselves humble will be made important."[203]

4.69 Jesus Teaches About Divorce

Some Pharisees came to Jesus. They tried to make him say something wrong. They asked him, "Is it right for a man to divorce his wife for any reason he chooses?"

Jesus answered, "Surely you have read this in the Scriptures: When God made the world, 'he made people male and female.' And God said, 'That is why a man will leave his father and mother and be joined to his wife. And the two people will become one.' So they are no longer two, but one. God has joined them together, so no one should separate them."

The Pharisees asked, "Then why did Moses give a command allowing a man to divorce his wife by writing a certificate of divorce?"

Jesus answered, "Moses allowed you to divorce your wives because you refused to accept God's teaching. But divorce was not allowed in the beginning. I tell you that whoever divorces his wife, except for the problem of sexual sin, and marries another woman is guilty of adultery."[204]

Later, when the followers and Jesus were in the house, they asked him again about the question of divorce. He said, "Whoever divorces his wife and marries another woman has sinned against his wife. He is guilty of adultery. And the woman who divorces her husband and marries another man is also guilty of adultery."[205]

The followers said to Jesus, "If that is the only reason a man can divorce his wife, it is better not to marry."

He answered, "This statement is true for some, but not for everyone—only for those who have been given this gift. There are different reasons why some men don't marry. Some were born without the ability to produce children. Others were made that way later in life. And others have given up marriage because of God's kingdom. This is for anyone who is able to accept it."[206]

4.70 Jesus Welcomes Children

People brought their small children to Jesus, so that he could lay his hands on them to bless them. But the followers told the people to stop bringing their children to him. Jesus saw what happened. He did not like his followers telling the children not to come. So he said to them, "Let the little children come to me. Don't stop them, because God's kingdom belongs to people who are like these little children. The truth is, you must accept God's kingdom like a little child accepts things, or you will never enter it." Then Jesus held the children in his arms. He laid his hands on them and blessed them.[207]

4.71 A Rich Man Refuses to Follow Jesus

A man came to Jesus and asked, "Teacher, what good thing must I do to have eternal life?"

Jesus answered, "Why do you ask me about what is good? Only God is good. But if you want to have eternal life, obey the law's commands."

The man asked, "Which ones?"

Jesus answered, "'You must not murder anyone, you must not commit adultery, you must not steal, you must not tell lies about others, you must respect your father and mother,' and 'love your neighbor the same as you love yourself.'"[208]

The man said, "Teacher, I have obeyed all these commands since I was a boy."

Jesus looked at the man in a way that showed how much he cared for him. He said, "There is still one thing you need to do.[209]

"If you want to be perfect, then go and sell all that you own. Give the money to the poor, and you will have riches in heaven. Then come and follow me!"

But when the young man heard Jesus tell him to give away his money, he was sad. He didn't want to do this, because he was very rich. So he left.

Then Jesus said to his followers, "The truth is, it will be very hard for a rich person to enter God's kingdom. Yes, I tell you, it is easier for a camel to go through the eye of a needle than for a rich person to enter God's kingdom."

The followers were amazed to hear this. They asked, "Then who can be saved?"

Jesus looked at them and said, "This is something that people cannot do. But God can do anything."

Peter said to him, "We left everything we had and followed you. So what will we have?"

Jesus said to them, "When the time of the new world comes, the Son of Man will sit on his great and glorious throne. And I can promise that you who followed me will sit on twelve thrones, and you will judge the twelve tribes of Israel. Everyone who has left houses, brothers, sisters, father, mother, children, or farms to follow me will get much more than they left. And they will have eternal life. Many people who are first now will be last in the future. And many who are last now will be first in the future."[210]

4.72 The Story About Workers in the Vineyard

"God's kingdom is like a man who owned some land. One morning, the man went out very early to hire some people to work in his vineyard. He agreed to pay the workers one silver coin for working that day. Then he sent them into the vineyard to work.

"About nine o'clock the man went to the marketplace and saw some other people standing there. They were doing nothing. So he said to them, 'If you go and work in my field, I will pay you what your work is worth.' So they went to work in the vineyard.

"The man went out again about twelve o'clock and again at three o'clock. Both times he hired some others to work in his vineyard. About five o'clock the man went to the marketplace again. He saw some other people standing there. He asked them, 'Why did you stand here all day doing nothing?'

"They said, 'No one gave us a job.'

"The man said to them, 'Then you can go and work in my vineyard.'

"At the end of the day, the owner of the field said to the boss of all the workers, 'Call the workers and pay them all. Start by paying the last people I hired. Then pay all of them, ending with the ones I hired first.'

"The workers who were hired at five o'clock came to get their pay. Each worker got one silver coin. Then the workers who were hired first came to get their pay. They thought they would be paid more than the others. But each one of them also received one silver coin. When they got their silver coin, they complained to the man who owned the land. They said, 'Those people were hired last and worked only one hour. But you paid them the same as us. And we worked hard all day in the hot sun.'

"But the man who owned the field said to one of them, 'Friend, I am being fair with you. You agreed to work for one silver coin. Right? So take your pay and go. I want to give the man who was hired last the same pay I gave you. I can do what I want with my own money. Why would you be jealous because I am generous?'

"So those who are last now will be first in the future. And those who are first now will be last in the future."²¹¹

4.73 Jesus Talks Again About His Death and Resurrection

Then Jesus talked to the twelve apostles alone. He said to them, "Listen, we are going to Jerusalem. Everything that God told the prophets to write about the Son of Man will happen. He will be handed over to the foreigners, who will laugh at him, insult him, and spit on him. They will beat him with whips and then kill him. But on the third day after his death, he will rise to life again." The apostles tried to understand this, but they could not; the meaning was hidden from them.²¹²

4.74 A Mother Asks a Special Favor

Then Zebedee's wife came to Jesus and brought her sons. She bowed before Jesus and asked him to do something for her.

Jesus said, "What do you want?"

She said, "Promise that one of my sons will sit at your right side in your kingdom and the other at your left."

So Jesus said to the sons, "You don't understand what you are asking. Can you drink from the cup that I must drink from?"

The sons answered, "Yes, we can!"

Jesus said to them, "It is true that you will drink from the cup that I drink from. But it is not for me to say who will sit at my right or my left. My Father has decided who will do that. He has prepared those places for them."

The other ten followers heard this and were angry with the two brothers. So Jesus called the followers together. He said, "You know that the rulers of the non-Jewish people love to show their power over the people. And their important leaders love to use all their authority over the people. But it should not be that way with you. Whoever wants to be your leader must be your servant. Whoever wants to be first must serve the rest of you like a slave. Do as I did: The Son of Man did not come for people to serve him. He came to serve others and to give his life to save many people."²¹³

4.75 Jesus Heals a Blind Man Named Bartimaeus

Then they came to the town of Jericho. When Jesus left there with his followers, a large crowd was with them. A blind man named Bartimaeus (meaning "son of Timaeus") was sitting by the road. He was always begging for money. He heard that Jesus from Nazareth was walking by. So he began shouting, "Jesus, Son of David, please help me!"

Many people criticized the blind man and told him to be quiet. But he shouted more and more, "Son of David, please help me!"

Jesus stopped and said, "Tell him to come here."

So they called the blind man and said, "You can be happy now. Stand up! Jesus is calling you." The blind man stood up quickly. He left his coat there and went to Jesus.

Jesus asked the man, "What do you want me to do for you?"

He answered, "Teacher, I want to see again."

Jesus said, "Go. You are healed because you believed." Immediately the man was able to see again. He followed Jesus down the road.[214]

4.76 Zacchaeus the Tax Collector

Jesus was going through the city of Jericho. In Jericho there was a man named Zacchaeus. He was a wealthy, very important tax collector. He wanted to see who Jesus was. There were many others who wanted to see Jesus too. Zacchaeus was too short to see above the people. So he ran to a place where he knew Jesus would come. Then he climbed a sycamore tree so he could see him.

When Jesus came to where Zacchaeus was, he looked up and saw him in the tree. Jesus said, "Zacchaeus, hurry! Come down! I must stay at your house today."

Zacchaeus hurried and came down. He was happy to have Jesus in his house. Everyone saw this. They began to complain, "Look at the kind of man Jesus is staying with. Zacchaeus is a sinner!"

Zacchaeus said to the Lord, "I want to do good. I will give half of my money to the poor. If I have cheated anyone, I will pay them back four times more."

Jesus said, "Today is the day for this family to be saved from sin. Yes, even this tax collector is one of God's chosen people. The Son of Man came to find lost people and save them."[215]

4.77 The Story About the Ten Servants

As the crowd listened to what he was saying, Jesus went on to tell a story. He was now near Jerusalem and knew that the people thought it was almost time for God's kingdom to come. So he said, "A very important man was preparing to go to a country far away to be made a king. Then he planned to return home and rule his people. So he called ten of his servants together. He gave a bag of money to each servant. He said, 'Do business with this money until I come back.' But the people in the kingdom hated the man. They sent a group to follow him to the other country. There they said, 'We don't want this man to be our king.'

"But the man was made king. When he came home, he said, 'Call those servants who have my money. I want to know how much more money they earned with it.' The first servant came and said, 'Sir, I earned ten bags of money with the one bag you gave me.' The king said to him, 'That's great! You are a good servant. I see that I can trust you with small things. So now I will let you rule over ten of my cities.'

"The second servant said, 'Sir, with your one bag of money I earned five bags.' The king said to this servant, 'You can rule over five cities.'

"Then another servant came in and said to the king, 'Sir, here is your bag of money. I wrapped it in a piece of cloth and hid it. I was afraid of you because you are a hard man. You even take money that you didn't earn and gather food that you didn't grow.'

"Then the king said to him, 'What a bad servant you are! I will use your own words to condemn you. You said that I am a hard man. You said that I even take money that I didn't earn and gather food that I didn't grow. If that is true, you should have put my money in the bank. Then, when I came back, my money would have earned some interest.' Then the king said to the men who were watching, 'Take the bag of money away from this servant and give it to the servant who earned ten bags of money.'

"The men said to the king, 'But sir, that servant already has ten bags of money.'

"The king said, 'People who use what they have will get more. But those who do not use what they have will have everything taken away from them. Now where are my enemies? Where are the people who did not want me to be king? Bring my enemies here and kill them. I will watch them die.'"

After Jesus said these things, he continued traveling toward Jerusalem.[216]

4.78 Mary Pours Perfume on Jesus at Bethany

It was almost time for the Jewish Passover festival. Many people from the country went to Jerusalem before the Passover. They went to do the special things to make themselves pure for the festival. The people looked for Jesus. They stood in the Temple area and asked each other, "Is he coming to the festival? What do you think?"

But the leading priests and the Pharisees had given a special order about Jesus. They said that anyone who knew where he was must tell them so that they could arrest him.

Six days before the Passover festival, Jesus went to Bethany. That is where Lazarus lived, the man Jesus raised from death. There they had a dinner for Jesus[217] at the house of Simon the leper.[218] Martha served the food, and Lazarus was one of the people eating with Jesus.

Mary brought in a pint of expensive perfume made of pure nard. She poured the perfume on Jesus' feet. Then she wiped his feet with her hair. And the sweet smell from the perfume filled the whole house.

Judas Iscariot, one of Jesus' followers, was there—the one who would later hand Jesus over to his enemies. Judas said, "That perfume was worth a full year's pay. It should have been sold, and the money should have been given to the poor people." But Judas did not really care about the poor. He said this because he was a thief. He was the one who kept the money bag for the group of followers. And he often stole money from the bag.[219]

Jesus said, "Leave her alone. Why are you giving her such trouble? She did a very good thing for me. You will always have the poor with you, and you can help them any time you want. But you will not always have me. This woman did the only thing she could do for me. She poured perfume on my body before I die to prepare it for burial. The Good News will be told to people all over the world. And I can assure you that everywhere the Good News is told, the story of what this woman did will also be told, and people will remember her."[220]

Many of the Jews heard that Jesus was in Bethany, so they went there to see him. They also went there to see Lazarus, the one Jesus raised from death. So the leading priests made plans to kill Lazarus too. Because of him, many Jews were leaving them and believing in Jesus. That is why they wanted to kill Lazarus too.[221]

5 The Week Jesus Dies

5.1 *Jesus Enters Jerusalem*
The next day the people in Jerusalem heard that Jesus was coming there. These were the crowds of people who had come to the Passover festival.[222]

He came near Bethphage and Bethany, towns near the hill called the Mount of Olives. He sent out two of his followers. He said, "Go into the town you can see there. When you enter the town, you will find a young donkey tied there that no one has ever ridden. Untie it, and bring it here to me. If anyone asks you why you are taking the donkey, you should say, 'The Master needs it.'"

The two followers went into town. They found the donkey exactly like Jesus told them. They untied it, but its owners came out. They said to the followers, "Why are you untying our donkey?"

The followers answered, "The Master needs it." So the followers brought the donkey to Jesus. They put their coats on its back. Then they put Jesus on the donkey. He rode along the road toward Jerusalem.[223]

Many people spread their coats on the road for Jesus. Others cut branches in the fields and spread the branches on the road. Some of them were walking ahead of Jesus. Others were walking behind him. Everyone shouted,

"'Praise Him!'
  'Welcome! God bless the one who comes in the name of the
      Lord!'

"God bless the kingdom of our father David.
    That kingdom is coming!
  Praise to God in heaven!"[224]

Jesus was coming close to Jerusalem. He was already near the bottom of the Mount of Olives. The whole group of followers was happy. They were very excited and praised God. They thanked God for all the powerful things they had seen. They said,

"'Welcome! God bless the king who comes in the name of the Lord.'

Peace in heaven and glory to God!"

Some of the Pharisees said to Jesus, "Teacher, tell your followers not to say these things."
But Jesus answered, "I tell you, if my followers didn't say them, these stones would shout them."
Jesus came near Jerusalem. Looking at the city, he began to cry for it and said, "I wish you knew today what would bring you peace. But it is hidden from you now. A time is coming when your enemies will build a wall around you and hold you in on all sides. They will destroy you and all your people. Not one stone of your buildings will stay on top of another. All this will happen because you did not know the time when God came to save you."[225]
Then Jesus went into Jerusalem. All the people in the city were confused. They asked, "Who is this man?"
The crowds following Jesus answered, "This is Jesus. He is the prophet from the town of Nazareth in Galilee."[226]
Some blind people and some who were crippled came to Jesus in the Temple area. Jesus healed them. The leading priests and the teachers of the law saw the wonderful things he was doing. And they saw the children praising him in the Temple area. The children were shouting, "Praise to the Son of David." All this made the priests and the teachers of the law angry.
They asked Jesus, "Do you hear what these children are saying?"
He answered, "Yes. The Scriptures say, 'You have taught children and babies to give praise.' Have you not read that Scripture?"
Then Jesus left them and went out of the city to Bethany, where he spent the night.[227]

5.2 Jesus Says a Fig Tree Will Die
The next day, Jesus was leaving Bethany. He was hungry. He saw a fig tree with leaves. So he went to the tree to see if it had any figs

growing on it. But he found no figs on the tree. There were only leaves, because it was not the right time for figs to grow. So Jesus said to the tree, "People will never eat fruit from you again." His followers heard him say this.[228]

5.3 Jesus Forces Merchants Out of the Temple

Jesus went to Jerusalem and entered the Temple area. He began driving out the people who were buying and selling things there. He turned over the tables that belonged to those who were exchanging different kinds of money. And he turned over the benches of those who were selling doves. He refused to allow anyone to carry things through the Temple area. Then Jesus began teaching the people and said, "It is written in the Scriptures, 'My Temple will be called a house of prayer for all nations.' But you have changed it into a 'hiding place for thieves.'"[229]

Jesus taught the people in the Temple area every day. The leading priests, the teachers of the law, and some of the leaders of the people wanted to kill him. But they did not know how they could do it, because everyone was listening to him. The people were very interested in what Jesus said.[230]

5.4 Jesus Talks About His Death Again

There were some Greeks there too. These were some of the people who went to Jerusalem to worship at the Passover festival. They went to Philip, who was from Bethsaida in Galilee. They said, "Sir, we want to meet Jesus." Philip went and told Andrew. Then Andrew and Philip went and told Jesus.

Jesus said to them, "The time has come for the Son of Man to receive his glory. It is a fact that a grain of wheat must fall to the ground and die before it can grow and produce much more wheat. If it never dies, it will never be more than a single seed. Whoever loves the life they have now will lose it. But whoever is willing to give up their life in this world will keep it. They will have eternal life. Whoever serves me must follow me. My servants must be with me everywhere I am. My Father will give honor to anyone who serves me.

"Now I am very troubled. What should I say? Should I say, 'Father save me from this time of suffering'? No, I came to this time so that I could suffer. Father, do what will bring you glory!"

Then a voice came from heaven, "I have already brought glory to myself. I will do it again."

The people standing there heard the voice. They said it was thunder.

But others said, "An angel spoke to him!"

Jesus said, "That voice was for you and not for me. Now is the time for the world to be judged. Now the ruler of this world will be thrown out. I will be lifted up from the earth. When that happens, I will draw all people to myself." Jesus said this to show how he would die.

The people said, "But our law says that the Messiah will live forever. So why do you say, 'The Son of Man must be lifted up'? Who is this 'Son of Man'?"

Then Jesus said, "The light will be with you for only a short time more. So walk while you have the light. Then the darkness will not catch you. People who walk in the darkness don't know where they are going. So put your trust in the light while you still have it. Then you will be children of light."[231]

5.5 Some Jews Refuse to Believe in Jesus

When Jesus finished saying these things, he went away to a place where the people could not find him.

The people saw all these miraculous signs Jesus did, but they still did not believe in him. This was to give full meaning to what Isaiah the prophet said:

"Lord, who believed what we told them?
　　Who has seen the Lord's power?"

This is why the people could not believe. Because Isaiah also said,

"God made the people blind.
　　He closed their minds.
He did this so that they would not see with their eyes and
　　understand with their minds.
He did it so that they would not turn and be healed."

Isaiah said this because he saw Jesus' divine greatness. So he spoke about him.

But many people believed in Jesus. Even many of the Jewish leaders believed in him, but they were afraid of the Pharisees, so they did not say openly that they believed. They were afraid they would be ordered to stay out of the synagogue. They loved praise from people more than praise from God.

Then Jesus said loudly, "Everyone who believes in me is really believing in the one who sent me. Everyone who sees me is really seeing the one who sent me. I came into this world as a light. I came so that everyone who believes in me will not stay in darkness.

"I did not come into the world to judge people. I came to save the people in the world. So I am not the one who judges those who hear my teaching and do not obey. But there is a judge for all those who refuse to believe in me and do not accept what I say. The message I have spoken will judge them on the last day. That is because what I taught was not from myself. The Father who sent me told me what to say and what to teach. And I know that whatever he says to do will bring eternal life. So the things I say are exactly what the Father told me to say."[232]

That night Jesus and his followers left the city.[233]

5.6 The Fig Tree Is Dry and Dead

The next morning Jesus was walking with his followers. They saw the fig tree that he spoke to the day before. The tree was dry and dead, even the roots. Peter remembered the tree and said to Jesus, "Teacher, look! Yesterday, you told that fig tree to die. Now it is dry and dead!"

Jesus answered, "Have faith in God. The truth is, you can say to this mountain, 'Go, mountain, fall into the sea.' And if you have no doubts in your mind and believe that what you say will happen, then God will do it for you. So I tell you to ask for what you want in prayer. And if you believe that you have received those things, then they will be yours. When you are praying, and you remember that you are angry with another person about something, then forgive that person. Forgive them so that your Father in heaven will also forgive your sins."[234]

5.7 Religious Leaders Doubt Jesus' Authority

Jesus and his followers went again to Jerusalem. Jesus was walking in the Temple area. The leading priests, the teachers of the law, and the older Jewish leaders came to him. They said, "Tell us! What authority do you have to do these things? Who gave you this authority?"

Jesus answered, "I will ask you a question. You answer my question. Then I will tell you whose authority I use to do these things. Tell me: When John baptized people, did his authority come from God or was it only from other people? Answer me."

These Jewish leaders talked about Jesus' question. They said to each other, "If we answer, 'John's baptism was from God,' then he will say, 'Then why didn't you believe John?' But we can't say that John's baptism was from someone else." (These leaders were afraid of the people, because the people believed that John was a prophet.)

So the leaders answered Jesus, "We don't know the answer."

Jesus said, "Then I will not tell you who gave me the authority to do these things."[235]

5.8 The Story About the Two Sons

"Tell me what you think about this: There was a man who had two sons. He went to the first son and said, 'Son, go and work today in the vineyard.'

"The son answered, 'I will not go.' But later he decided he should go, and he went.

"Then the father went to the other son and said, 'Son, go and work today in the vineyard.' He answered, 'Yes, sir, I will go and work.' But he did not go.

"Which of the two sons obeyed his father?"

The Jewish leaders answered, "The first son."

Jesus said to them, "The truth is, you are worse than the tax collectors and the prostitutes. In fact, they will enter God's kingdom before you enter. John came showing you the right way to live, and you did not believe him. But the tax collectors and prostitutes believed John. You saw that happening, but you would not change. You still refused to believe him."[236]

5.9 The Story About the Wicked Farmers

"Listen to this story: There was a man who owned a vineyard. He put a wall around the field and dug a hole for a winepress. Then he built a tower.[237] He leased the land to some farmers and then left on a trip.

"Later, it was time for the grapes to be picked. So the man sent a servant to the farmers to get his share of the grapes. But the farmers grabbed the servant and beat him. They sent him away with nothing. Then the man sent another servant to the farmers. They hit this servant on the head, showing no respect for him. So the man sent another servant. The farmers killed this servant. The man sent many other servants to the farmers. The farmers beat some of them and killed the others.

"The man had only one person left to send to the farmers. It was his son. He loved his son, but he decided to send him. He said, 'The farmers will respect my son.'

"But the farmers said to each other, 'This is the owner's son, and this vineyard will be his. If we kill him, it will be ours.' So they took the son, threw him out of the vineyard, and killed him.[238]

"So what will the owner of the vineyard do to these farmers when he comes?"

The Jewish priests and leaders said, "He will surely kill those evil men. Then he will lease the land to other farmers, who will give him his share of the crop at harvest time."

Jesus said to them, "Surely you have read this in the Scriptures:

'The stone that the builders refused to accept became the
 cornerstone.
The Lord did this, and it is wonderful to us.'

"So I tell you that God's kingdom will be taken away from you. It will be given to people who do what God wants in his kingdom. Whoever falls on this stone will be broken. And it will crush anyone it falls on."

When the leading priests and the Pharisees heard these stories, they knew that Jesus was talking about them. They wanted to find a way to arrest Jesus. But they were afraid to do anything, because the people believed that Jesus was a prophet.[239]

5.10 *The Story About the Wedding Feast*

Jesus used some more stories to teach the people. He said, "God's kingdom is like a king who prepared a wedding feast for his son. He invited some people to the feast. When it was ready, the king sent his servants to tell the people to come. But they refused to come to the king's feast.

"Then the king sent some more servants. He said to them, 'I have already invited the people. So tell them that my feast is ready. I have killed my best bulls and calves to be eaten. Everything is ready. Come to the wedding feast.'

"But when the servants told the people to come, they refused to listen. They all went to do other things. One went to work in his field, and another went to his business. Some of the other people grabbed the servants, beat them, and killed them. The king was very angry. He sent his army to kill those who murdered his servants. And the army burned their city.

"After that, the king said to his servants, 'The wedding feast is ready. I invited those people, but they were not good enough to come to my feast. So go to the street corners and invite everyone you see. Tell them to come to my feast.' So the servants went into the streets. They gathered all the people they could find, good and bad alike, and brought them to where the wedding feast was ready. And the place was filled with guests.

"When the king came in to meet the guests, he saw a man there who was not dressed in the right clothes for a wedding. The king said, 'Friend, how were you allowed to come in here? You are not wearing the right clothes.' But the man said nothing. So the king told some servants, 'Tie this man's hands and feet. Throw him out into the darkness, where people are crying and grinding their teeth with pain.'

"Yes, many people are invited. But only a few are chosen."[240]

5.11 Is It Right to Pay Taxes to Caesar or Not?

Then the Pharisees left the place where Jesus was teaching. They made plans to catch him saying something wrong. They sent some men to Jesus. They were some of their own followers and some from the group called Herodians. They said, "Teacher, we know you are an honest man. We know you teach the truth about God's way. You are not afraid of what others think about you. All people are the same to you. So tell us what you think. Is it right to pay taxes to Caesar or not?"

But Jesus knew that these men were trying to trick him. So he said, "You hypocrites! Why are you trying to catch me saying something wrong? Show me a coin used for paying the tax." They showed Jesus a silver coin. Then he asked, "Whose picture is on the coin? And whose name is written on the coin?"

They answered, "It is Caesar's picture and Caesar's name."

Then Jesus said to them, "Give to Caesar what belongs to Caesar, and give to God what belongs to God."

When they heard what Jesus said, they were amazed. They left him and went away.[241]

5.12 Marriage and the Seven Brothers

That same day some Sadducees came to Jesus. (Sadducees believe that no one will rise from death.) The Sadducees asked Jesus a question. They said, "Teacher, Moses told us that if a married man dies and had no children, his brother must marry the woman. Then they will have children for the dead brother. There were seven brothers among us. The first brother married but died. He had no children. So his brother married the woman. Then the second brother also died. The same thing happened to the third brother and all the other brothers. The woman was the last to die. But all seven men had married her. So when people rise from death, whose wife will she be?"

Jesus answered, "You are so wrong! You don't know what the Scriptures say. And you don't know anything about God's power. At the time when people rise from death, there will be no marriage. People will not be married to each other. Everyone will be like the angels in heaven. Surely you have read what God said to you about people rising from death. God said, 'I am the God of Abraham, the God of Isaac, and the God of Jacob.' So they were not still dead, because he is the God only of living people."

When the people heard this, they were amazed at Jesus' teaching.[242]

5.13 The Most Important Command

The Pharisees learned that Jesus had made the Sadducees look so foolish that they stopped trying to argue with him. So the Pharisees had a meeting. Then one of them, an expert in the Law of Moses, asked Jesus a question to test him. He said, "Teacher, which command in the law is the most important?"[243]

Jesus answered, "The most important command is this: 'People of Israel, listen! The Lord our God is the only Lord. Love the Lord your God with all your heart, all your soul, all your mind, and all your strength.' The second most important command is this: 'Love your neighbor the same as you love yourself.' These two commands are the most important.[244]

"All of the law and the writings of the prophets take their meaning from these two commands."[245]

The man answered, "That was a good answer, Teacher. You are right in saying that God is the only Lord and that there is no other God. And you must love God with all your heart, all your mind, and all your strength. And you must love others the same as you love yourself. These commands are more important than all the animals and sacrifices we offer to God."

Jesus saw that the man answered him wisely. So he said to him, "You are close to God's kingdom."[246]

5.14 Is the Messiah David's Son or David's Lord?

So while the Pharisees were together, Jesus asked them a question. He said, "What do you think about the Messiah? Whose son is he?"

The Pharisees answered, "The Messiah is the Son of David."

Jesus said to them, "Then why did David call him 'Lord'? David was speaking by the power of the Spirit. He said,

'The Lord God said to my Lord:
 Sit by me at my right side,
   and I will put your enemies under your control.'

David calls the Messiah 'Lord.' So how can he be David's son?" None of the Pharisees could answer Jesus' question. And after that day, no one was brave enough to ask him any more questions.[247]

5.15 Jesus Criticizes the Religious Leaders

Then Jesus spoke to the people and to his followers. He said, "The teachers of the law and the Pharisees have the authority to tell you what the Law of Moses says. So you should obey them. Do everything they tell you to do. But their lives are not good examples for you to follow. They tell you to do things, but they don't do those things themselves. They make strict rules that are hard for people to obey. They try to force others to obey all their rules. But they themselves will not try to follow any of those rules.

"The only reason they do what they do is for other people to see them. They make the little Scripture boxes they wear bigger and bigger. And they make the tassels on their prayer clothes long enough for people to notice them. These men love to have the places of honor at banquets and the most important seats in the synagogues. They love for people to show respect to them in the marketplaces and to call them 'Teacher.'

"But you must not be called 'Teacher.' You are all equal as brothers and sisters. You have only one Teacher. And don't call anyone on earth 'Father.' You have one Father. He is in heaven. And you should not be called 'Master.' You have only one Master, the Messiah. Whoever serves you like a servant is the greatest among you. People who think they are better than others will be made humble. But people who humble themselves will be made great.

"It will be bad for you teachers of the law and you Pharisees! You are hypocrites! You close the way for people to enter God's kingdom. You yourselves don't enter, and you stop those who are trying to enter.

"It will be bad for you teachers of the law and you Pharisees! You are hypocrites. You travel across the seas and across different countries to find one person who will follow your ways. When you find that person, you make him worse than you are. And you are so bad that you belong in hell!

"It will be bad for you teachers of the law and you Pharisees! You guide the people, but you are blind. You say, 'If anyone uses the name of the Temple to make a promise, that means nothing. But anyone who uses the gold that is in the Temple to make a promise must keep that promise.' You are blind fools! Can't you see that the Temple is greater than the gold on it? It's the Temple that makes the gold holy!

"And you say, 'If anyone uses the altar to make a promise, that means nothing. But anyone who uses the gift on the altar to make a promise must keep that promise.' You are blind! Can't you see that the altar is greater than any gift on it? It's the altar that makes the gift holy! Whoever uses the altar to make a promise is really using the altar and everything on the altar. And anyone who uses the Temple to make a promise is really using the Temple and God, who lives in it. Whoever uses heaven to make a promise is using God's throne and the one who is seated on it.

"It will be bad for you teachers of the law and you Pharisees! You are hypocrites! You give God a tenth of the food you get, even your mint, dill, and cumin. But you don't obey the really important teachings of the law—being fair, showing mercy, and being faithful. These are the things you should do. And you should also continue to do those other things. You guide the people, but you are blind! Think about a man picking a little fly out of his drink and then swallowing a camel! You are like that.

"It will be bad for you teachers of the law and you Pharisees! You are hypocrites! You wash clean the outside of your cups and dishes. But inside they are full of what you got by cheating others and pleasing yourselves. Pharisees, you are blind! First make the inside of the cup clean and good. Then the outside of the cup will also be clean.

"It will be bad for you teachers of the law and you Pharisees! You are hypocrites! You are like tombs that are painted white. Outside they look fine, but inside they are full of dead people's bones and all kinds of filth. It is the same with you. People look at you and think you are godly. But on the inside you are full of hypocrisy and evil.

"It will be bad for you teachers of the law and you Pharisees! You are hypocrites! You build tombs for the prophets. And you show honor to the graves of the godly people who were killed. And you say, 'If we had lived during the time of our ancestors, we would not have helped them kill these prophets.' So you give proof that you are descendants of those who killed the prophets. And you will finish the sin that your ancestors started!

"You are snakes! You are from a family of poisonous snakes! You will not escape God. You will all be judged guilty and go to hell! So I tell you this: I send to you prophets and teachers who are wise and know the Scriptures. You will kill some of them. You will hang some of them on crosses. You will beat some of them in your synagogues. You will chase them from town to town.

"So you will be guilty for the death of all the good people who have been killed on earth. You will be guilty for the killing of that godly man Abel. And you will be guilty for the killing of Zechariah son of Berachiah. He was killed between the Temple and the altar. You will be guilty for the killing of all the good people who lived between the time of Abel and the time of Zechariah. Believe me when I say that all of these things will happen to you people who are living now.

"O Jerusalem, Jerusalem! You kill the prophets. You stone to death those that God has sent to you. Many, many times I wanted to help your people. I wanted to gather them together as a hen gathers her chicks under her wings. But you did not let me. Now your house will be left completely empty. I tell you, you will not see me again until that time when you will say, 'Welcome! God bless the one who comes in the name of the Lord.'"[248]

5.16 A Poor Widow Gives All She Has

Jesus sat near the Temple collection box and watched as people put money into it. Many rich people put in a lot of money. Then a poor widow came and put in two very small copper coins, worth less than a penny.

Jesus called his followers to him and said, "This poor widow put in only two small coins. But the truth is, she gave more than all those rich people. They have plenty, and they gave only what they did not need. This woman is very poor, but she gave all she had. It was money she needed to live on."[249]

5.17 Jesus Warns About the Future

Jesus was leaving the Temple area. One of his followers said to him, "Teacher, look how big those stones are! What beautiful buildings!"

Jesus said, "Do you see these great buildings? They will all be destroyed. Every stone will be thrown down to the ground. Not one stone will be left on another."

Later, Jesus was sitting at a place on the Mount of Olives. He was alone with Peter, James, John, and Andrew. They could all see the Temple, and they said to Jesus, "Tell us when these things will happen. And what will show us it is time for them to happen?"

Jesus said to them, "Be careful! Don't let anyone fool you. Many people will come and use my name. They will say, 'I am the one' and will fool many people. You will hear about wars that are being fought. And you will hear stories about other wars beginning. But don't be afraid. These things must happen before the end comes. Nations will fight against other nations. Kingdoms will fight against other kingdoms. There will be times when there is no food for people to eat. And there will be earthquakes in different places. These things are only the beginning of troubles, like the first pains of a woman giving birth.

"You must be careful! There are people who will arrest you and take you to be judged for being my followers. They will beat you in their synagogues. You will be forced to stand before kings and governors. You will tell them about me. Before the end comes, the Good News must be told to all nations. Even when you are arrested and put on trial, don't worry about what you will say. Say whatever God tells you at the time. It will not really be you speaking. It will be the Holy Spirit.

"Brothers will turn against their own brothers and hand them over to be killed. Fathers will hand over their own children to be killed. Children will fight against their own parents and have them killed. All people will hate you because you follow me. But those who remain faithful to the end will be saved.[250]

Many false prophets will come and cause many people to believe things that are wrong. There will so much more evil in the world that the love of most believers will grow cold. But the one who remains faithful to the end will be saved. And the Good News I have shared about God's kingdom will be told throughout the world. It will be spread to every nation. Then the end will come.

"Daniel the prophet spoke about 'the terrible thing that causes destruction.' You will see this terrible thing standing in the holy place." (You who read this should understand what it means.) "The people in Judea at that time should run away to the mountains. They should run away without wasting time to stop for anything. If they are on the roof of their house, they must not go down to get anything out of the house. If they are in the field, they must not go back to get a coat.

"During that time it will be hard for women who are pregnant or have small babies! Pray that it will not be winter or a Sabbath day when these things happen and you have to run away, because it will be a time of great trouble. There will be more trouble than has ever happened since the beginning of the world. And nothing as bad as that will ever happen again.

"But God has decided to make that terrible time short. If it were not made short, no one would continue living. But God will make that time short to help the people he has chosen.

"Someone might say to you at that time, 'Look, there is the Messiah!' Or someone else might say, 'There he is!' But don't believe them. False Messiahs and false prophets will come and do great miracles and wonders, trying to fool the people God has chosen, if that is possible. Now I have warned you about this before it happens.

"Someone might tell you, 'The Messiah is there in the desert!' But don't go into the desert to look for him. Someone else might say, 'There is the Messiah in that room!' But don't believe it. When the Son of Man comes, everyone will see him. It will be like lightning flashing in the sky that can be seen everywhere. It's like looking for a dead body: You will find it where the vultures are gathering above.

"Right after the trouble of those days, this will happen:

'The sun will become dark,
  and the moon will not give light.
The stars will fall from the sky,
  and everything in the sky will be changed.'

"Then there will be something in the sky that shows the Son of Man is coming. All the people of the world will cry. Everyone will see the Son of Man coming on the clouds in the sky. He will come with power and great glory. He will use a loud trumpet to send his angels all around the earth. They will gather his chosen people from every part of the earth.[251]

"When these things begin to happen, stand up tall and don't be afraid. Know that it is almost time for God to free you!"

Then Jesus told this story: "Look at all the trees. The fig tree is a good example. When it turns green, you know that summer is near. In the same way, when you see all these things happening, you will know that God's kingdom is coming very soon.

"I assure you that all these things will happen while some of the people of this time are still living. The whole world, earth and sky, will be destroyed, but my words will last forever."[252]

5.18 Only God Knows When the Time Will Be

"No one knows when that day or time will be. The Son and the angels in heaven don't know when it will be. Only the Father knows.

"When the Son of Man comes, it will be the same as what happened during Noah's time. In those days before the flood, people were eating and drinking, marrying and giving their children to be married right up to the day Noah entered the boat. They knew nothing about what was happening until the flood came and destroyed them all.

"It will be the same when the Son of Man comes. Two men will be working together in the field. One will be taken and the other will be left. Two women will be grinding grain with a mill. One will be taken and the other will be left.[253]

"Be careful not to spend your time having parties and getting drunk or worrying about this life. If you do that, you won't be able to think straight, and the end might come when you are not ready. It will come as a surprise to everyone on earth. So be ready all the time. Pray that you will be able to get through all these things that will happen and stand safe before the Son of Man."[254]

"It's like a man who goes on a trip and leaves his house in the care of his servants. He gives each one a special job to do. He tells the servant guarding the door to always be ready. And this is what I am telling you now. You must always be ready. You don't know when the owner of the house will come back. He might come in the afternoon, or at midnight, or in the early morning, or when the sun rises. If you are always ready, he will not find you sleeping, even if he comes back earlier than expected. I tell you this, and I say it to everyone: 'Be ready!'"[255]

"Obviously, a homeowner who knew what time a thief was planning to come would be ready and not let the thief break in. So you also must be ready. The Son of Man will come at a time when you don't expect him.

"Who is the wise and trusted servant? The master trusts one servant to give the other servants their food at the right time. Who is the one the master trusts to do that work? When the master comes and finds that servant doing the work he gave him, what a great day it will be for that servant. I can tell you without a doubt, the master will choose that servant to take care of everything he owns.

But what will happen if that servant is evil and thinks his master will not come back soon? He will begin to beat the other servants. He will eat and drink with others who are drunk. Then the master will come when the servant is not ready, at a time when the servant is not expecting him. Then the master will punish that servant. He will send him away to be with the hypocrites, where people will cry and grind their teeth with pain."[256]

5.19 *The Story About the Ten Girls*

"At that time God's kingdom will be like ten girls who went to wait for the bridegroom. They took their lamps with them. Five of the girls were foolish, and five were wise. The foolish girls took their lamps with them, but they did not take extra oil for the lamps. The wise girls took their lamps and more oil in jars. When the bridegroom was very late, the girls could not keep their eyes open, and they all fell asleep.

"At midnight someone announced, 'The bridegroom is coming! Come and meet him!'

"Then all the girls woke up. They made their lamps ready. But the foolish girls said to the wise girls, 'Give us some of your oil. The oil in our lamps is all gone.'

"The wise girls answered, 'No! The oil we have might not be enough for all of us. But go to those who sell oil and buy some for yourselves.'

"So the foolish girls went to buy oil. While they were gone, the bridegroom came. The girls who were ready went in with the bridegroom to the wedding feast. Then the door was closed and locked.

"Later, the other girls came. They said, 'Sir, sir! Open the door to let us in.'

"But the bridegroom answered, 'Certainly not! I don't even know you.'

"So always be ready. You don't know the day or the time when the Son of Man will come."[257]

5.20 The Story About the Three Servants

"At that time God's kingdom will also be like a man leaving home to travel to another place for a visit. Before he left, he talked with his servants. He told his servants to take care of his things while he was gone. He decided how much each servant would be able to care for. The man gave one servant five bags of money. He gave another servant two bags. And he gave a third servant one bag. Then he left. The servant who got five bags went quickly to invest the money. Those five bags of money earned five more. It was the same with the servant who had two bags. That servant invested the money and earned two more. But the servant who got one bag of money went away and dug a hole in the ground. Then he hid his master's money in the hole.

"After a long time the master came home. He asked the servants what they did with his money. The servant who got five bags brought that amount and five more bags of money to the master. The servant said, 'Master, you trusted me to care for five bags of money. So I used them to earn five more.'

"The master answered, 'You did right. You are a good servant who can be trusted. You did well with that small amount of money. So I will let you care for much greater things. Come and share my happiness with me.'

"Then the servant who got two bags of money came to the master. The servant said, 'Master, you gave me two bags of money to care for. So I used your two bags to earn two more.'

"The master answered, 'You did right. You are a good servant who can be trusted. You did well with a small amount of money. So I will let you care for much greater things. Come and share my happiness with me.'

"Then the servant who got one bag of money came to the master. The servant said, 'Master, I knew you were a very hard man. You harvest what you did not plant. You gather crops where you did not put any seed. So I was afraid. I went and hid your money in the ground. Here is the one bag of money you gave me.'

"The master answered, 'You are a bad and lazy servant! You say you knew that I harvest what I did not plant and that I gather crops where I did not put any seed. So you should have put my money in the bank. Then, when I came home, I would get my money back. And I would also get the interest that my money earned.'

"So the master told his other servants, 'Take the one bag of money from that servant and give it to the servant who has ten bags. Everyone who uses what they have will get more. They will have much more than they need. But people who do not use what they have will have everything taken away from them.' Then the master said, 'Throw that useless servant outside into the darkness, where people will cry and grind their teeth with pain.'"[258]

5.21 *The Son of Man Will Judge All People*

"The Son of Man will come again with divine greatness, and all his angels will come with him. He will sit as king on his great and glorious throne. All the people of the world will be gathered before him. Then he will separate everyone into two groups. It will be like a shepherd separating his sheep from his goats. He will put the sheep on his right and the goats on his left.

"Then the king will say to the godly people on his right, 'Come, my Father has great blessings for you. The kingdom he promised is now yours. It has been prepared for you since the world was made. It is yours because when I was hungry, you gave me food to eat. When I was thirsty, you gave me something to drink. When I had no place to stay, you welcomed me into your home. When I was without clothes, you gave me something to wear. When I was sick, you cared for me. When I was in prison, you came to visit me.'

"Then the godly people will answer, 'Lord, when did we see you hungry and give you food? When did we see you thirsty and give you something to drink? When did we see you with no place to stay and welcome you into our home? When did we see you without clothes and give you something to wear? When did we see you sick or in prison and care for you?'

"Then the king will answer, 'The truth is, anything you did for any of my people here, you also did for me.'

"Then the king will say to the evil people on his left, 'Get away from me. God has already decided that you will be punished. Go into the fire that burns forever—the fire that was prepared for the devil and his angels. You must go away because when I was hungry, you gave me nothing to eat. When I was thirsty, you gave me nothing to drink. When I had no place to stay, you did not welcome me into your home. When I was without clothes, you gave me nothing to wear. When I was sick and in prison, you did not care for me.'

"Then those people will answer, 'Lord, when did we see you hungry or thirsty? When did we see you without a place to stay? Or when did we see you without clothes or sick or in prison? When did we see any of this and not help you?'

"The king will answer, 'The truth is, anything you refused to do for any of my people here, you refused to do for me.'

"Then these evil people will go away to be punished forever. But the godly people will go and enjoy eternal life."[259]

5.22 *The Plan to Kill Jesus*

After Jesus finished saying all these things, he said to his followers, "You know that the day after tomorrow is Passover. On that day the Son of Man will be handed over to his enemies to be killed on a cross."

Then the leading priests and the older Jewish leaders had a meeting at the palace where the high priest lived. The high priest's name was Caiaphas. In the meeting they tried to find a way to arrest and kill Jesus without anyone knowing what they were doing. They planned to arrest Jesus and kill him. They said, "We cannot arrest Jesus during Passover. We don't want the people to become angry and cause a riot."[260]

5.23 Judas Agrees to Help Jesus' Enemies

One of Jesus' twelve apostles was named Judas Iscariot. Satan entered him, and he went and talked with the leading priests and some of the soldiers who guarded the Temple. He talked to them about a way to hand Jesus over to them.[261]

He said, "I will hand Jesus over to you. What will you pay me for doing this?" The priests gave him 30 silver coins. After that, Judas waited for the best time to hand Jesus over to them.[262]

5.24 Preparations for the Passover Meal

The Day of Unleavened Bread came. This was the day when the Jews always killed the lambs for the Passover. Jesus said to Peter and John, "Go and prepare the Passover meal for us to eat."

They said to him, "Where do you want us to prepare the meal?"

He said to them, "When you go into the city, you will see a man carrying a jar of water. Follow him. He will go into a house. Tell the owner of the house, 'The Teacher asks that you please show us the room where he and his followers can eat the Passover meal.' Then the owner will show you a large room upstairs that is ready for us. Prepare the meal there."

So Peter and John left. Everything happened the way Jesus said. So they prepared the Passover meal.[263]

Jesus' Last Supper with His Followers (5.25–40)

5.25 Who Is the Most Important?

When time came for them to eat the Passover meal,[264] the apostles began to argue about which one of them was the most important. But Jesus said to them, "The kings of the world rule over their people, and those who have authority over others want to be called 'the great providers for the people.' But you must not be like that. The one with the most authority among you should act as if he is the least important. The one who leads should be like one who serves. Who is more important: the one serving or the one sitting at the table being served?

Everyone thinks it's the one being served, right? But I have been with you as the one who serves.

"You men have stayed with me through many struggles. So I give you authority to rule with me in the kingdom the Father has given me. You will eat and drink at my table in that kingdom. You will sit on thrones and judge the twelve tribes of Israel."[265]

5.26 Jesus Washes His Followers' Feet

The Father had given Jesus power over everything. Jesus knew this. He also knew that he had come from God. And he knew that he was going back to God. So while they were eating, Jesus stood up and took off his robe. He got a towel and wrapped it around his waist. Then he poured water into a bowl and began to wash the followers' feet. He dried their feet with the towel that was wrapped around his waist.

He came to Simon Peter. But Peter said to him, "Lord, you should not wash my feet."

Jesus answered, "You don't know what I am doing now. But later you will understand."

Peter said, "No! You will never wash my feet."

Jesus answered, "If I don't wash your feet, you are not one of my people."

Simon Peter said, "Lord, after you wash my feet, wash my hands and my head too!"

Jesus said, "After a person has a bath, his whole body is clean. He needs only to wash his feet. And you are clean, but not all of you." Jesus knew who would hand him over to his enemies. That is why he said, "Not all of you are clean."

When Jesus finished washing their feet, he put on his clothes and went back to the table. He asked, "Do you understand what I did for you? You call me 'Teacher.' And you call me 'Lord.' And this is right, because that is what I am. I am your Lord and Teacher. But I washed your feet. So you also should wash each other's feet. I did this as an example for you. So you should serve each other just as I served you. Believe me, servants are not greater than their master. Those who are sent to do something are not greater than the one who sent them. If you know these things, you will be happy if you do them."[266]

5.27 Jesus Tells Who Will Turn Against Him

"I am not talking about all of you. I know the people I have chosen. But what the Scriptures say must happen: 'The man who shared my food has turned against me.' I am telling you this now before it happens. Then when it happens, you will believe that I AM. I assure you, whoever accepts the person I send also accepts me. And whoever accepts me also accepts the one who sent me."[267]

Jesus said to them, "I wanted very much to eat this Passover meal with you before I die. I will never eat another Passover meal until it is given its full meaning in God's kingdom."[268]

They were all eating. Then Jesus said, "Believe me when I say that one of you twelve here will hand me over to my enemies."[269]

His followers all looked at each other. They did not understand who Jesus was talking about.[270]

The followers were very sad to hear this. Each one said, "Lord, surely I am not the one!"[271]

One of the followers was next to Jesus and was leaning close to him. This was the one Jesus loved very much. Simon Peter made signs to this follower to ask Jesus who he was talking about.

That follower leaned closer to Jesus and asked, "Lord, who is it?"

Jesus answered him, "I will dip this bread into the dish. The man I give it to is the one.[272]

"The Son of Man will suffer what the Scriptures say will happen to him. But it will be very bad for the one who hands over the Son of Man to be killed. It would be better for him if he had never been born."

Then Judas, the very one who would hand him over, said to Jesus, "Teacher, surely I am not the one you are talking about, am I?"[273]

So Jesus took a piece of bread, dipped it, and gave it to Judas Iscariot, the son of Simon. When Judas took the bread, Satan entered him. Jesus said to Judas, "What you will do—do it quickly!" No one at the table understood why Jesus said this to Judas. Since Judas was the one in charge of the money, some of them thought that Jesus meant for him to go and buy some things they needed for the feast. Or they thought that Jesus wanted him to go give something to the poor.

Judas ate the bread Jesus gave him. Then he immediately went out. It was night.[274]

5.28 The New Agreement From God

Then Jesus took a cup of wine. He gave thanks to God for it and said, "Take this cup and give it to everyone here. I will never drink wine again until God's kingdom comes."[275]

While they were eating, Jesus took some bread and thanked God for it. He broke off some pieces, gave them to his followers and said, "Take this bread and eat it. It is my body[276] that I am giving for you. Eat this to remember me."

In the same way, after supper, Jesus took the cup of wine[277] thanked God for it, and gave it to them. He said, "Each one of you drink some of it.[278] This wine represents the new agreement from God to his people. It will begin when my blood is poured out for you.[279] It will be poured out to forgive the sins of many and begin the new agreement from God to his people. I want you to know, I will not drink this wine again until that day when we are together in my Father's kingdom and the wine is new. Then I will drink it again with you."[280]

5.29 Jesus Gives a New Command

When Judas was gone, Jesus said, "Now is the time for the Son of Man to receive his glory. And God will receive glory through him. If God receives glory through him, he will give glory to the Son through himself. And that will happen very soon."

Jesus said, "My children, I will be with you only a short time more. You will look for me, but I tell you now what I told the Jewish leaders: Where I am going you cannot come.

"I give you a new command: Love each other. You must love each other just as I loved you. All people will know that you are my followers if you love each other."[281]

5.30 Jesus Says Peter Will Deny Him

Simon Peter asked Jesus, "Lord, where are you going?"

Jesus answered, "Where I am going you cannot follow now. But you will follow later."

Peter asked, "Lord, why can't I follow you now? I am ready to die for you!"

Jesus answered, "Will you really give your life for me? The truth is, before the rooster crows, you will say three times that you don't know me."[282]

Jesus told the followers, "Tonight you will all lose your faith in me. The Scriptures say,

'I will kill the shepherd,
  and the sheep will run away.'

But after I am killed, I will rise from death. Then I will go into Galilee. I will be there before you go there."

Peter answered, "All the other followers may lose their faith in you. But my faith will never be shaken."[283]

"Satan has asked to test you men like a farmer tests his wheat. O Simon, Simon, I have prayed that you will not lose your faith! Help your brothers be stronger when you come back to me."

But Peter said to Jesus, "Lord, I am ready to go to jail with you. I will even die with you!"[284]

Jesus answered, "Will you really give your life for me? The truth is,[285] tonight you will say you don't know me. You will say it three times before the rooster crows twice."

But Peter strongly protested, "I will never say I don't know you! I will even die with you!" And all the other followers said the same thing.[286]

Then Jesus said to the apostles, "Remember when I sent you out without money, a bag, or sandals? Did you need anything?"

The apostles said, "No."

Jesus said to them, "But now if you have money or a bag, carry that with you. If you don't have a sword, sell your coat and buy one. The Scriptures say,

'He was considered a criminal.'

This Scripture must happen. It was written about me, and it is happening now."

The followers said, "Look, Lord, here are two swords."

Jesus said to them, "That's enough."[287]

5.31 Jesus Comforts His Followers

Jesus said, "Don't be troubled. Trust in God, and trust in me. There are many rooms in my Father's house. I would not tell you this if it were not true. I am going there to prepare a place for you. After I go and prepare a place for you, I will come back. Then I will take you with me, so that you can be where I am. You know the way to the place where I am going."[288]

5.32 Jesus Is the Only Way to the Father

Thomas said, "Lord, we don't know where you are going, so how can we know the way?"

Jesus answered, "I am the way, the truth, and the life. The only way to the Father is through me. If you really knew me, you would know my Father too. But now you know the Father. You have seen him."

Philip said to him, "Lord, show us the Father. That is all we need."

Jesus answered, "Philip, I have been with you for a long time. So you should know me. Anyone who has seen me has seen the Father too. So why do you say, 'Show us the Father'? Don't you believe that I am in the Father and the Father is in me? The things I have told you don't come from me. The Father lives in me, and he is doing his own work. Believe me when I say that I am in the Father and the Father is in me. Or believe because of the miracles I have done.

"I can assure you that whoever believes in me will do the same things I have done. And they will do even greater things than I have done, because I am going to the Father. And if you ask for anything in my name, I will do it for you. Then the Father's glory will be shown through the Son. If you ask me for anything in my name, I will do it."[289]

5.33 Jesus Promises the Holy Spirit

"If you love me, you will do what I command. I will ask the Father, and he will give you another Helper to be with you forever. The Helper is the Spirit of truth. The people of the world cannot accept him, because they don't see him or know him. But you know him. He lives with you, and he will be in you.

"I will not leave you all alone like orphans. I will come back to you. In a very short time the people in the world will not see me anymore. But you will see me. You will live because I live. On that day you will know that I am in the Father. You will know that you are in me and I am in you. Those who really love me are the ones who not only know my commands but also obey them. My Father will love such people, and I will love them. I will make myself known to them."

Then Judas (not Judas Iscariot) said, "Lord, how will you make yourself known to us, but not to the world?"

Jesus answered, "All who love me will obey my teaching. My Father will love them. My Father and I will come to them and live with them. But anyone who does not love me does not obey my teaching. This teaching that you hear is not really mine. It is from my Father who sent me.

"I have told you all these things while I am with you. But the Helper will teach you everything and cause you to remember all that I told you. This Helper is the Holy Spirit that the Father will send in my name.

"I leave you peace. It is my own peace I give you. I give you peace in a different way than the world does. So don't be troubled. Don't be afraid. You heard me say to you, 'I am leaving, but I will come back to you.' If you loved me, you would be happy that I am going back to the Father, because the Father is greater than I am. I have told you this now, before it happens. Then when it happens, you will believe.

"I will not talk with you much longer. The ruler of this world is coming. He has no power over me. But the world must know that I love the Father. So I do exactly what the Father told me to do.

"Come now, let's go."[290]

5.34 Jesus Is Like a Vine

Jesus said, "I am the true vine, and my Father is the gardener. He cuts off every branch of mine that does not produce fruit. He also trims every branch that produces fruit to prepare it to produce even more. You have already been prepared to produce more fruit by the teaching I have given you. Stay joined to me and I will stay joined to you. No branch can produce fruit alone. It must stay connected to the vine. It is the same with you. You cannot produce fruit alone. You must stay joined to me.

"I am the vine, and you are the branches. If you stay joined to me, and I to you, you will produce plenty of fruit. But separated from me you won't be able to do anything. If you don't stay joined to me, you will be like a branch that has been thrown out and has dried up. All the dead branches like that are gathered up, thrown into the fire and burned. Stay joined together with me, and follow my teachings. If you do this, you can ask for anything you want, and it will be given to you. Show that you are my followers by producing much fruit. This will bring honor to my Father.

"I have loved you as the Father has loved me. Now continue in my love. I have obeyed my Father's commands, and he continues to love me. In the same way, if you obey my commands, I will continue to love you. I have told you these things so that you can have the true happiness that I have. I want you to be completely happy. This is what I command you: Love each other as I have loved you. The greatest love people can show is to die for their friends. You are my friends if you do what I tell you to do. I no longer call you servants, because servants don't know what their master is doing. But now I call you friends, because I have told you everything that my Father told me.

"You did not choose me. I chose you. And I gave you this work: to go and produce fruit—fruit that will last. Then the Father will give you anything you ask for in my name. This is my command: Love each other."[291]

5.35 Jesus Warns His Followers

"If the world hates you, remember that they hated me first. If you belonged to the world, the world would love you as it loves its own people. But I have chosen you to be different from those in the world. So you don't belong to the world, and that is why the world hates you.

"Remember the lesson I told you: Servants are not greater than their master. If people treated me badly, they will treat you badly too. And if they obeyed my teaching, they will obey yours too. They will do to you whatever they did to me, because you belong to me. They don't know the one who sent me. If I had not come and spoken to the people of the world, they would not be guilty of sin. But now I have spoken to them. So they have no excuse for their sin.

"Whoever hates me also hates my Father. I did things among the people of the world that no one else has ever done. If I had not done those things, they would not be guilty of sin. But they have seen what I did, and still they hate me and my Father. But this happened to make clear the full meaning of what is written in their law: 'They hated me for no reason.'

"I will send you the Helper from the Father. The Helper is the Spirit of truth who comes from the Father. When he comes, he will tell about me. And you will tell people about me too, because you have been with me from the beginning. "I have told you all this so that you won't lose your faith when you face troubles. People will tell you to leave their synagogues and never come back. In fact, the time will come when they will think that killing you would be doing service for God. They will do this because they have not known the Father, and they have not known me. I have told you all this now to prepare you. So when the time comes for these things to happen, you will remember that I warned you."[292]

5.36 The Work of the Holy Spirit

"I did not tell you these things at the beginning, because I was with you then. Now I am going back to the one who sent me. And none of you asks me, 'Where are you going?' But you are filled with sadness because I have told you all this. Let me assure you, it is better for you that I go away. I say this because when I go away I will send the Helper to you. But if I did not go, the Helper would not come.

"When the Helper comes, he will show the people of the world how wrong they are about sin, about being right with God, and about judgment. He will prove that they are guilty of sin, because they don't believe in me. He will show them how wrong they are about how to be right with God. The Helper will do this, because I am going to the Father. You will not see me then. And he will show them how wrong their judgment is, because their leader has already been condemned.

"I have so much more to tell you, but it is too much for you to accept now. But when the Spirit of truth comes, he will lead you into all truth. He will not speak his own words. He will speak only what he hears and will tell you what will happen in the future. The Spirit of truth will bring glory to me by telling you what he receives from me. All that the Father has is mine. That is why I said that the Spirit will tell you what he receives from me."[293]

5.37 Sadness Will Turn Into Happiness

"After a short time you won't see me. Then after another short time you will see me again."

Some of the followers said to each other, "What does he mean when he says, 'After a short time you won't see me. Then after another short

The Week Jesus Dies

time you will see me again'? And what does he mean when he says, 'Because I am going to the Father'?" They also asked, "What does he mean by 'a short time'? We don't understand what he is saying."

Jesus saw that the followers wanted to ask him about this. So he said to them, "Are you asking each other what I meant when I said, 'After a short time you won't see me. Then after another short time you will see me again'? The truth is, you will cry and be sad, but the world will be happy. You will be sad, but then your sadness will change to happiness.

"When a woman gives birth to a baby, she has pain, because her time has come. But when her baby is born, she forgets the pain. She forgets because she is so happy that a child has been born into the world. It is the same with you. Now you are sad, but I will see you again, and you will be happy. You will have a joy that no one can take away. In that day you will not have to ask me about anything. And I assure you, my Father will give you anything you ask him for in my name. You have never asked for anything in this way before. But ask in my name, and you will receive. And you will have the fullest joy possible.

"I have told you these things, using words that hide the meaning. But the time will come when I will not use words like that to tell you things. I will speak to you in plain words about the Father. Then you will be able to ask the Father for things in my name. I'm not saying that I will have to ask the Father for you. The Father himself loves you because you have loved me. And he loves you because you have believed that I came from God. I came from the Father into the world. Now I am leaving the world and going back to the Father."

Then his followers said, "You are already speaking plainly to us. You are not using words that hide the meaning. We can see now that you know all things. You answer our questions even before we ask them. This makes us believe that you came from God."

Jesus said, "So now you believe? Listen to me. A time is coming when you will be scattered, each to his own home. In fact, that time is already here. You will leave me, and I will be alone. But I am never really alone, because the Father is with me.

"I have told you these things so that you can have peace in me. In this world you will have troubles. But be brave! I have defeated the world!"[294]

5.38 Jesus Talks to His Father

After Jesus said these things, he looked toward heaven and prayed, "Father, the time has come. Give glory to your Son so that the Son can give glory to you. You gave the Son power over all people so that he could give eternal life to all those you have given to him. And this is eternal life: that people can know you, the only true God, and that they can know Jesus Christ, the one you sent. I finished the work you gave me to do. I brought you glory on earth. And now, Father, give me glory with you. Give me the glory I had with you before the world was made."[295]

5.39 Jesus Prays for His Followers

"You gave me some people from the world. I have shown them what you are like. They belonged to you, and you gave them to me. They have obeyed your teaching. Now they know that everything I have came from you. I told them the words you gave me, and they accepted them. They realized the fact that I came from you and believed that you sent me. I pray for them now. I am not praying for the people in the world. But I am praying for these people you gave me, because they are yours. All I have is yours, and all you have is mine. And my glory is seen in them.

"Now I am coming to you. I will not stay in the world, but these followers of mine are still in the world. Holy Father, keep them safe by the power of your name—the name you gave me. Then they will be one, just as you and I are one. While I was with them, I kept them safe by the power of your name—the name you gave me. I protected them. And only one of them was lost—the one who was sure to be lost. This was to show the truth of what the Scriptures said would happen.

"I am coming to you now. But I pray these things while I am still in the world. I say all this so that these followers can have the true happiness that I have. I want them to be completely happy. I have given them your teaching. And the world has hated them, because they don't belong to the world, just as I don't belong to the world.

"I am not asking you to take them out of the world. But I am asking that you keep them safe from the Evil One. They don't belong to the world, just as I don't belong to the world. Make them ready for your service through your truth. Your teaching is truth. I have sent them into the world, just as you sent me into the world. I am making myself completely ready to serve you. I do this for them, so that they also might be fully qualified for your service."[296]

5.40 Jesus Prays for All Who Will Believe in Him

"I pray not only for these followers but also for those who will believe in me because of their teaching. Father, I pray that all who believe in me can be one. You are in me and I am in you. I pray that they can also be one in us. Then the world will believe that you sent me. I have given them the glory that you gave me. I gave them this glory so that they can be one, just as you and I are one. I will be in them, and you will be in me. So they will be completely one. Then the world will know that you sent me and that you loved them just as you loved me.

"Father, I want these people you have given me to be with me in every place I am. I want them to see my glory—the glory you gave me because you loved me before the world was made. Father, you are the one who always does what is right. The world does not know you, but I know you, and these followers of mine know that you sent me. I showed them what you are like, and I will show them again. Then they will have the same love that you have for me, and I will live in them."[297]

5.41 Jesus Prays Alone

They all sang a song and then went out to the Mount of Olives.[298]

Then Jesus went with his followers to a place called Gethsemane. He said to them, "Sit here while I go there and pray." He told Peter and the two sons of Zebedee to come with him. Then he began to be very sad and troubled. Jesus said to Peter and the two sons of Zebedee, "My heart is so heavy with grief, I feel as if I am dying. Wait here and stay awake with me."

Then Jesus went on a little farther away from them. He fell to the ground and prayed, "My Father, if it is possible, don't make me drink from this cup. But do what you want, not what I want."[299]

Then an angel from heaven came to help him. Jesus was full of pain; he struggled hard in prayer. Sweat dripped from his face like drops of blood falling to the ground.[300]

Then he went back to his followers and found them sleeping. He said to Peter, "Could you men not stay awake with me for one hour? Stay awake and pray for strength against temptation. Your spirit wants

The Life and Teachings of Jesus of Nazareth

to do what is right, but your body is weak."

Then Jesus went away a second time and prayed, "My Father, if I must do this and it is not possible for me to escape it, then I pray that what you want will be done."

Then he went back to the followers. Again he found them sleeping. They could not stay awake. So he left them and went away one more time and prayed. This third time he prayed, he said the same thing.

Then Jesus went back to the followers and said, "Are you still sleeping and resting? The time has come for the Son of Man to be handed over to the control of sinful men. Stand up! We must go. Here comes the one who will hand me over."[301]

5.42 Jesus Is Arrested

Judas, the one responsible for handing Jesus over, knew where this place was. He knew because Jesus often met there with his followers. So Judas led a group of soldiers to the garden, along with some guards from the leading priests and the Pharisees. They were carrying torches, lanterns, and weapons.

Jesus already knew everything that would happen to him. So he went out and asked them, "Who are you looking for?"

They answered, "Jesus from Nazareth."

He said, "I am Jesus." (Judas, the one responsible for handing Jesus over, was standing there with them.) When Jesus said, "I am Jesus," the men moved back and fell to the ground.

He asked them again, "Who are you looking for?"

They said, "Jesus from Nazareth."

Jesus said, "I told you that I am Jesus. So if you are looking for me, let these other men go free." This was to show the truth of what Jesus said earlier: "I have not lost anyone you gave me."[302]

Judas planned to do something to show them which one was Jesus. He said, "The one I kiss will be Jesus. Arrest him." So he went to Jesus and said, "Hello, Teacher!" Then Judas kissed him.[303]

But Jesus said to him, "Judas, are you using the kiss of friendship to hand over the Son of Man to his enemies?"[304]

The men grabbed Jesus and arrested him.[305]

Simon Peter had a sword, which he pulled out. He struck the servant of the high priest and cut off his right ear. (The servant's name was Malchus.)[306]

Jesus said, "Stop!" Then he touched the servant's ear and healed him.[307]

Jesus said to Peter, "Put your sword back in its place![308] People who use swords will be killed with swords.[309]

"I must drink from the cup the Father has given me.[310]

"Surely you know I could ask my Father and he would give me more than twelve armies of angels. But it must happen this way to show the truth of what the Scriptures said."

Then Jesus said to the crowd, "Why do you come to get me with swords and clubs as if I were a criminal. Every day I sat in the Temple area teaching. You did not arrest me there. But all these things have happened to show the full meaning of what the prophets wrote." Then all of Jesus' followers left him and ran away.[311]

One of those following Jesus was a young man wearing only a linen cloth. When the people tried to grab him, he left the cloth in their hands and ran away naked.[312]

5.43 Jesus Is Brought Before Annas

Then the soldiers with their commander and the Jewish guards arrested Jesus. They tied him and brought him to Annas, the father-in-law of Caiaphas. Caiaphas was the high priest that year. He was also the one who had told the other Jewish leaders that it would be better if one man died for all the people.[313] So Annas sent Jesus to Caiaphas the high priest. He was still tied.[314]

The men who arrested Jesus led him to the house of Caiaphas the high priest. The teachers of the law and the older Jewish leaders were gathered there.[315]

5.44 Peter's First Denial of Jesus

Simon Peter and another one of Jesus' followers went with Jesus. This follower knew the high priest. So he went with Jesus into the yard of the high priest's house. But Peter waited outside near the door. The follower who knew the high priest came back outside and spoke to the gatekeeper. Then he brought Peter inside.[316]

It was cold, so the servants and guards had built a fire. They were standing around it, warming themselves, and Peter was standing with them.[317]

While Peter was still in the yard, a servant girl of the high priest came there.[318] She said to Peter, "Are you also one of the followers of that man?"[319] She looked closely at him and said, "You were with Jesus, that man from Nazareth."

But Peter said this was not true. "That makes no sense," he said. "I don't know what you are talking about!" Then he left and went to the entrance of the yard, and a rooster crowed.[320]

5.45 The High Priest Questions Jesus

The high priest asked Jesus questions about his followers and what he taught them. Jesus answered, "I have always spoken openly to all people. I always taught in the synagogues and in the Temple area. All the Jews come together there. I never said anything in secret. So why do you question me? Ask the people who heard my teaching. They know what I said."

When Jesus said this, one of the guards standing there hit him. The guard said, "You should not talk to the high priest like that!"

Jesus answered, "If I said something wrong, tell everyone here what was wrong. But if what I said is right, then why do you hit me?"[321]

5.46 Peter's Second and Third Denial

Simon Peter was standing at the fire, keeping himself warm. The other people said to Peter, "Aren't you one of the followers of that man?"[322]

When the servant girl saw him there, she began saying again to the people standing around, "This man is one of them." Again Peter said it was not true.

A short time later, the people standing there said, "We know you are one of them, because you are from Galilee."[323]

One of the servants of the high priest was there. He was a relative of the man whose ear Peter had cut off. The servant said, "I think I saw you with him in the garden!"[324]

Then Peter began to curse. He said, "I swear to God, I don't know this man you are talking about!"[325]

Immediately, while he was still speaking, a rooster crowed. Then the Lord turned and looked into Peter's eyes. And Peter remembered what the Lord had said, "Before the rooster crows in the morning, you will say three times that you don't know me." Then Peter went outside and cried bitterly.[326]

5.47 Jesus Before the High Council

The leading priests and the whole high council tried to find something that Jesus had done wrong so they could kill him. But the council could find no proof that would allow them to kill Jesus. Many people came and told lies against Jesus, but they all said different things. None of them agreed.[327]

Then two people came and said, "This man said, 'I can destroy the Temple of God and build it again in three days.'"[328]

"We heard this man say, 'I will destroy this Temple built by human hands. And three days later, I will build another Temple not made by human hands.'" But also what these people said did not agree.

Then the high priest stood up before everyone and said to Jesus, "These people said things against you. Do you have something to say about their charges? Are they telling the truth?" But Jesus said nothing to answer him. The high priest asked Jesus another question: "Are you the Messiah, the Son of the blessed God?"

Jesus answered, "Yes, I am the Son of God. And in the future you will see the Son of Man sitting at the right side of God All-Powerful. And you will see the Son of Man coming on the clouds of heaven."

When the high priest heard this, he tore his clothes in anger. He said, "We don't need any more witnesses! You all heard these insults to God. What do you think?" Everyone agreed that Jesus was guilty and must be killed.

Some of the people there spit at him. They covered his eyes and hit him with their fists. They said, "Be a prophet and tell us who hit you!" Then the guards led Jesus away and beat him.[329]

The next morning, the older leaders of the people, the leading priests, and the teachers of the law came together. They led Jesus away to their high council. They said, "If you are the Messiah, then tell us that you are."

Jesus said to them, "If I tell you I am the Messiah, you will not believe me. And if I ask you, you will not answer. But beginning now, the Son of Man will sit at the right side of God All-Powerful."

They all said, "Then are you the Son of God?" Jesus said to them, "You are right in saying that I am."

They said, "Why do we need witnesses now? We all heard what he said!"[330]

5.48 Judas Kills Himself

Early the next morning, all the leading priests and older leaders of the people met and decided to kill Jesus. They tied him, led him away, and handed him over to Pilate, the governor.

Judas saw that they had decided to kill Jesus. He was the one who had handed him over. When he saw what happened, he was very sorry for what he had done. So he took the 30 silver coins back to the priests and the older leaders. Judas said, "I sinned. I handed over to you an innocent man to be killed."

The Jewish leaders answered, "We don't care! That's a problem for you, not us."

So Judas threw the money into the Temple. Then he went out from there and hanged himself.

The leading priests picked up the silver coins in the Temple. They said, "Our law does not allow us to keep this money with the Temple money, because this money has paid for a man's death." So they decided to use the money to buy a field called Potter's Field. This field would be a place to bury people who died while visiting in Jerusalem. That is why that field is still called the Field of Blood. This showed the full meaning of what Jeremiah the prophet said,

"They took 30 silver coins. That was how much the people of Israel decided to pay for his life. They used those 30 silver coins to buy the potter's field, as the Lord commanded me."[331]

5.49 Jesus Is Brought Before Pilate

Then the guards took Jesus from Caiaphas' house to the Roman governor's palace. It was early in the morning. The Jews there would not go inside the palace. They did not want to make themselves unclean, because they wanted to eat the Passover meal. So Pilate went outside to them and asked, "What do you say this man has done wrong?"

They answered, "He is a bad man. That is why we brought him to you."

Pilate said to them, "You take him yourselves and judge him by your own law."

The Jewish leaders answered, "But your law does not allow us to punish anyone by killing them." (This was to show the truth of what Jesus said about how he would die.)

Then Pilate went back inside the palace. He called for Jesus and asked him, "Are you the king of the Jews?"

Jesus said, "Is that your own question, or did other people tell you about me?"

Pilate said, "I'm not a Jew! It was your own people and their leading priests who brought you before me. What have you done wrong?"

Jesus said, "My kingdom does not belong to this world. If it did, my servants would fight so that I would not be handed over to the Jewish leaders. No, my kingdom is not an earthly one."

Pilate said, "So you are a king."

Jesus answered, "You are right to say that I am a king. I was born for this: to tell people about the truth. That is why I came into the world. And everyone who belongs to the truth listens to me."

Pilate said, "What is truth?" Then he went out to the Jewish leaders again and said to them, "I can find nothing against this man."[332]

They began to accuse Jesus and said to Pilate, "We caught this man trying to change the thinking of our people. He says we should not pay taxes to Caesar. He calls himself the Messiah, a king."[333]

So Pilate asked Jesus another question. He said, "You can see that these people are accusing you of many things. Why don't you answer?"

But Jesus still did not answer, and this really surprised Pilate.[334]

But they kept on saying, "His teaching is causing trouble all over Judea. He began in Galilee, and now he is here!"

Pilate heard this and asked if Jesus was from Galilee. He learned that Jesus was under Herod's authority. Herod was in Jerusalem at that time, so Pilate sent Jesus to him.[335]

5.50 Pilate Sends Jesus to King Herod

When Herod saw Jesus, he was very happy. He had heard all about him and had wanted to meet him for a long time. Herod wanted to see a miracle, so he was hoping that Jesus would do one. He asked him many questions, but Jesus said nothing. The leading priests and teachers of the law were standing there shouting things against Jesus. Then Herod and his soldiers laughed at him. They made fun of him by dressing him in clothes like kings wear. Then Herod sent him back to Pilate. In the past Pilate and Herod had always been enemies. But on that day they became friends.[336]

5.51 Pilate Tries to Free Jesus

Every year at the Passover time the governor would free one prisoner—whichever one the people wanted. There was a man in prison at that time named Barabbas. He and the rebels with him had been put in prison for committing murder during a riot.

The people came to Pilate and asked him to free a prisoner as he always did.[337]

Pilate called all the people together with the leading priests and the Jewish leaders. He said to them, "You brought this man to me. You said he was trying to change the people. But I judged him before you all and have not found him guilty of the things you say he has done. Herod didn't find him guilty either. He sent him back to us. Look, he has done nothing bad enough for the death penalty.[338]

When a crowd gathered, Pilate said to them, "I will free one man for you. Which one do you want me to free: Barabbas or Jesus who is called the Messiah?" Pilate knew that they had handed Jesus over to him because they were jealous of him.

While Pilate was sitting there in the place for judging, his wife sent a message to him. It said, "Don't do anything with that man. He is not guilty. Last night I had a dream about him, and it troubled me very much."

But the leading priests and older Jewish leaders told the people to ask for Barabbas to be set free and for Jesus to be killed.

Pilate said, "I have Barabbas and Jesus. Which one do you want me to set free for you?"

The people answered, "Barabbas!"[339]

5.52 Jesus Is Handed Over to Be Crucified

Then Pilate ordered that Jesus be taken away and whipped. The soldiers made a crown from thorny branches and put it on his head. Then they put a purple robe around him. They kept coming up to him and saying, "Hail to the king of the Jews!" And they hit him in the face.

Again Pilate came out and said to the Jewish leaders, "Look! I am bringing Jesus out to you. I want you to know that I find nothing I can charge him with." Then Jesus came out wearing the crown of thorns and the purple robe. Pilate said to the Jews, "Here is the man!"

When the leading priests and the Jewish guards saw Jesus they shouted, "Kill him on a cross! Kill him on a cross!"

But Pilate answered, "You take him and nail him to a cross yourselves. I find nothing I can charge him with."

The Jewish leaders answered, "We have a law that says he must die, because he said he is the Son of God."

When Pilate heard this, he was more afraid. So he went back inside the palace and asked Jesus, "Where are you from?" But Jesus did not answer him. Pilate said, "You refuse to speak to me? Remember, I have the power to make you free or to kill you on a cross."

Jesus answered, "The only power you have over me is the power given to you by God. So the one who handed me over to you is guilty of a greater sin."

After this, Pilate tried to let Jesus go free. But the Jewish leaders shouted, "Anyone who makes himself a king is against Caesar. So if you let this man go free, that means you are not Caesar's friend."

When Pilate heard this, he brought Jesus out to the place called "The Stone Pavement." (In Aramaic the name is *Gabbatha*.) Pilate sat down on the judge's seat there. It was now almost noon on Preparation day of Passover week. Pilate said to the Jews, "Here is your king!"

They shouted, "Take him away! Take him away! Kill him on a cross!"

Pilate asked them, "Do you want me to kill your king on a cross?"

The leading priests answered, "The only king we have is Caesar!"[340]

Pilate saw that there was nothing he could do to make the people change. In fact, it looked as if there would be a riot. So he took some water and washed his hands in front of them all. He said, "I am not guilty of this man's death. You are the ones who are doing it!"

The people answered, "We will take full responsibility for his death. You can blame us and even our children!"[341]

Pilate decided to give them what they wanted. They wanted Barabbas to go free—the one who was in jail for starting a riot and for murder. Pilate let Barabbas go free. And he handed Jesus over to be killed. This is what the people wanted.[342]

5.53 Pilate's Soldiers Make Fun of Jesus

Then Pilate's soldiers took Jesus into the governor's palace. All the soldiers gathered around him. They took off Jesus' clothes and put a red robe on him. Then they made a crown from thorny branches and put it on his head, and they put a stick in his right hand. Then they bowed before him, making fun of him. They said, "We salute you, king of the Jews!" They spit on him. Then they took his stick and kept hitting him on the head with it. After they finished making fun of him, the soldiers took off the robe and put his own clothes on him again. Then they led him away to be killed on a cross.[343]

5.54 Jesus Is Nailed to a Cross

The soldiers led Jesus away. At that same time there was a man from Cyrene named Simon coming into the city from the fields. The soldiers forced him to carry Jesus' cross and walk behind him.

A large crowd followed Jesus. Some of the women were sad and crying. They felt sorry for him. But Jesus turned and said to the women, "Women of Jerusalem, don't cry for me. Cry for yourselves and for your children too. The time is coming when people will say, 'The women who cannot have babies are the ones God has blessed. It's really a blessing that they have no children to care for.' Then the people will say to the mountains, 'Fall on us!' They will say to the hills, 'Cover us!' If this can happen to someone who is good, what will happen to those who are guilty?"

There were also two criminals led out with Jesus to be killed.[344]

They came to the place called Golgotha. (Golgotha means "The Place of the Skull.") There the soldiers gave Jesus some wine mixed with gall. But when he tasted it, he refused to drink it.[345]

They were led to a place called "The Skull." There the soldiers nailed Jesus to the cross. They also nailed the criminals to crosses beside Jesus—one on the right and the other on the left.

Jesus said, "Father, forgive them. They don't know what they are doing."[346]

After the soldiers nailed Jesus to the cross, they took his clothes and divided them into four parts. Each soldier got one part. They also took his tunic. It was all one piece of cloth woven from top to bottom. So the soldiers said to each other, "We should not tear this into parts. Let's throw lots to see who will get it." This happened to make clear the full meaning of what the Scriptures say:

"They divided my clothes among them,
 and they threw lots for what I was wearing."

So the soldiers did this.[347]

Pilate told them to write a sign and put it on the cross. The sign said, "JESUS OF NAZARETH, THE KING OF THE JEWS." The sign was written in Aramaic, in Latin, and in Greek.

Many of the Jews read this sign, because the place where Jesus was nailed to the cross was near the city. The leading Jewish priests said to Pilate, "Don't write, 'The King of the Jews.' But write, 'This man said, I am the King of the Jews.'"

Pilate answered, "I will not change what I have written."[348]

People walked by and shouted insults at Jesus. They shook their heads and said, "You said you could destroy the Temple and build it again in three days. So save yourself! Come down from that cross if you really are the Son of God!"

The leading priests, the teachers of the law, and the older Jewish leaders were also there. They made fun of Jesus the same as the other people did. They said, "He saved others, but he can't save himself! People say he is the king of Israel. If he is the king, he should come down now from the cross. Then we will believe in him. He trusted God. So let God save him now, if God really wants him. He himself said, 'I am the Son of God.'"[349]

One of the criminals hanging there began to shout insults at Jesus: "Aren't you the Messiah? Then save yourself, and save us too!"

But the other criminal stopped him. He said, "You should fear God. All of us will die soon. You and I are guilty. We deserve to die because we did wrong. But this man has done nothing wrong." Then he said, "Jesus, remember me when you begin ruling as king!"

Then Jesus said to him, "I promise you, today you will be with me in paradise."[350]

Jesus' mother stood near his cross. Her sister was also standing there with Mary the wife of Clopas, and Mary Magdalene. Jesus saw his mother. He also saw the follower he loved very much standing there. He said to his mother, "Dear woman, here is your son." Then he said to the follower, "Here is your mother." So after that, this follower took Jesus' mother to live in his home.[351]

5.55 Jesus Dies

At noon the whole country became dark. The darkness continued for three hours. About three o'clock Jesus cried out loudly, "*Eli, Eli, lema sabachthani?*" This means "My God, my God, why have you left me alone?"

Some of the people standing there heard this. They said, "He is calling Elijah."[352]

Later, Jesus knew that everything had been done. To make the Scriptures come true he said, "I am thirsty." There was a jar full of sour wine there, so the soldiers soaked a sponge in it. They put the sponge on a branch of a hyssop plant and lifted it to Jesus' mouth. When he tasted the wine, he said, "It is finished."[353]

Jesus shouted, "Father, I put my life in your hands!" After Jesus said this, he died.[354]

When Jesus died, the curtain in the Temple was torn into two pieces. The tear started at the top and tore all the way to the bottom. Also, the earth shook and rocks were broken. The graves opened, and many of God's people who had died were raised from death. They came out of the graves. And after Jesus was raised from death, they went into the holy city, and many people saw them.

The army officer and the soldiers guarding Jesus saw this earthquake and everything that happened. They were very afraid and said, "He really was the Son of God!"[355]

This day was Preparation day. The next day was a special Sabbath day. The Jewish leaders did not want the bodies to stay on the cross on the Sabbath day. So they asked Pilate to order that the legs of the men be broken. And they asked that the bodies be taken down from the crosses. So the soldiers came and broke the legs of the two men on the crosses beside Jesus. But when the soldiers came close to Jesus, they saw that he was already dead. So they did not break his legs.

But one of the soldiers stuck his spear into Jesus' side. Immediately blood and water came out. (The one who saw this happen has told about it. He told about it so that you also can believe. The things he says are true. He knows that he tells the truth.) These things happened to give full meaning to the Scriptures that said, "None of his bones will be broken" and "People will look at the one they stabbed."[356]

5.56 Jesus Is Buried

Later, a man named Joseph from Arimathea asked Pilate for the body of Jesus. (Joseph was a follower of Jesus, but he did not tell anyone, because he was afraid of the Jewish leaders.) Pilate said Joseph could take Jesus' body, so he came and took it away.

Nicodemus went with Joseph. He was the man who had come to Jesus before and talked to him at night. He brought about 100 pounds of spices—a mixture of myrrh and aloes. These two men took Jesus' body and wrapped it in pieces of linen cloth with the spices. (This is how the Jews bury people.)[357]

He put Jesus' body in a new tomb that he had dug in a wall of rock. Then he closed the tomb by rolling a very large stone to cover the entrance. After he did this, he went away.[358]

Mary Magdalene and Mary the mother of Joses saw the place where Jesus was put.[359]

Then they left to prepare some sweet-smelling spices to put on the body.

On the Sabbath day they rested, as commanded in the Law of Moses.[360]

5.57 The Tomb of Jesus Is Guarded

That day was the day called Preparation day. The next day, the leading priests and the Pharisees went to Pilate. They said, "Sir, we remember that while that liar was still alive he said, 'I will rise from death in three days.' So give the order for the tomb to be guarded well for three days. His followers might come and try to steal the body. Then they could tell everyone that he has risen from death. That lie will be even worse than what they said about him before."

Pilate said, "Take some soldiers and go guard the tomb the best way you know." So they all went to the tomb and made it safe from thieves. They did this by sealing the stone in the entrance and putting soldiers there to guard it.[361]

6 The Last Forty Days

6.1 The Resurrection of Jesus

The next day after the Sabbath day,[362] suddenly an angel of the Lord came from the sky, and there was a huge earthquake. The angel went to the tomb and rolled the stone away from the entrance. Then he sat on top of the stone. The angel was shining as bright as lightning. His clothes were as white as snow. The soldiers guarding the tomb were very afraid of the angel. They shook with fear and then became like dead men.[363]

Mary Magdalene, Salome, and Mary the mother of James bought some sweet-smelling spices to put on Jesus' body. Very early on that day, the first day of the week, the women were going to the tomb. It was very early after sunrise. The women said to each other, "There is a large stone covering the entrance of the tomb. Who will move the stone for us?" Then the women looked and saw that the stone was moved. The stone was very large, but it was moved away from the entrance.[364]

They went in, but they did not find the body of the Lord Jesus. They did not understand this. While they were wondering about it, two men in shining clothes stood beside them. The women were very afraid. They bowed down with their faces to the ground.[365]

But the man said, "Don't be afraid. You are looking for Jesus from Nazareth, the one who was killed on a cross."[366]

The men said to them, "Why are you looking for a living person here? This is a place for dead people.[367] He has risen from death! He is not here. Look, here is the place they put him when he was dead.[368] Jesus is not here. He has risen from death. Do you remember what he said in Galilee? He said the Son of Man must be handed over to the control of sinful men, be killed on a cross, and rise from death on the third day.[369]

"Now go and tell his followers. And be sure to tell Peter. Tell them,

'Jesus is going into Galilee and will be there before you come. You will see him there, as he told you before.'"[370]

Then the women remembered what Jesus had said.[371]

So the women left the tomb quickly. They were afraid, but they were also very happy. They ran to tell his followers what happened.[372]

These women were Mary Magdalene, Joanna, Mary, the mother of James, and some others. They told the apostles everything that happened. But the apostles did not believe what they said. It sounded like nonsense.

But[373] Peter and the other follower started going to the tomb. They were both running, but the other follower ran faster than Peter and reached the tomb first. He bent down and looked in. He saw the pieces of linen cloth lying there, but he did not go in.

When Simon Peter finally reached the tomb, he went in and saw the pieces of linen lying there. He also saw the cloth that had been around Jesus' head. It was folded up and laid in a different place from the pieces of linen. Then the other follower went in—the one who had reached the tomb first. He saw what had happened and believed. (These followers did not yet understand from the Scriptures that Jesus must rise from death.) Then the followers went back home.[374]

6.2 Jesus Appears to Mary Magdalene

Jesus rose from death early on the first day of the week. He first appeared to Mary Magdalene. One time in the past Jesus had forced seven demons out of Mary.[375]

But Mary stood outside the tomb, crying. While she was crying, she bent down and looked inside the tomb. She saw two angels dressed in white sitting where Jesus' body had been. One was sitting where the head had been; the other was sitting where the feet had been.

The angels asked Mary, "Woman, why are you crying?"

Mary answered, "They took away the body of my Lord, and I don't know where they put him." When Mary said this, she turned around and saw Jesus standing there. But she did not know that it was Jesus.

He asked her, "Woman, why are you crying? Who are you looking for?"

She thought that this was the man who takes care of the garden. So she said to him, "Did you take him away, sir? Tell me where you put him. I will go and get him."

Jesus said to her, "Mary."

She turned toward him and said in Aramaic, "*Rabboni.*" (This means "Teacher.")

Jesus said to her, "You don't need to hold on to me! I have not yet gone back up to the Father. But go to my followers and tell them this: 'I am going back to my Father and your Father. I am going back to my God and your God.'"

Mary Magdalene went to the followers and told them, "I saw the Lord!" And she told them what he had said to her.[376]

But Mary told them that Jesus was alive. She said that she had seen Jesus, but they did not believe her.[377]

6.3 Jesus Appears to Others

Suddenly, Jesus was there in front of them. He said, "Hello!" The women went to him and, holding on to his feet, worshiped him. Then Jesus said to them, "Don't be afraid. Go tell my followers to go to Galilee. They will see me there."[378]

6.4 The Guards Report to the Religious Leaders

The women went to tell the followers. At the same time, some of the soldiers who were guarding the tomb went into the city. They went to tell the leading priests everything that happened. Then the priests met with the older Jewish leaders and made a plan. They paid the soldiers a lot of money and said to them, "Tell the people that Jesus' followers came during the night and stole the body while you were sleeping. If the governor hears about this, we will talk to him and keep you out of trouble." So the soldiers kept the money and obeyed the priests. And that story is still spread among the Jews even today.[379]

6.5 On the Road to Emmaus

That same day two of Jesus' followers were going to a town named Emmaus. It is about seven miles from Jerusalem. They were talking about everything that had happened. While they were talking, discussing these things, Jesus himself came near and walked with them. (But the two men were not allowed to recognize Jesus.) He asked them, "What's this I hear you discussing with each other as you walk?"

The two men stopped, their faces looking very sad. The one named Cleopas said, "You must be the only person in Jerusalem who doesn't know what has just happened there."

Jesus said, "What are you talking about?"

They said, "It's about Jesus, the one from Nazareth. To God and to all the people he was a great prophet. He said and did many powerful things. But our leaders and the leading priests handed him over to be judged and killed. They nailed him to a cross. We were hoping that he would be the one to free Israel. But then all this happened.

"And now something else: It has been three days since he was killed, but today some of our women told us an amazing thing. Early this morning they went to the tomb where the body of Jesus was laid. But they did not find his body there. They came and told us they had seen some angels in a vision. The angels told them Jesus was alive! So some of our group went to the tomb too. It was just like the women said. They saw the tomb, but they did not see Jesus."

Then Jesus said to the two men, "You are foolish and slow to realize what is true. You should believe everything the prophets said. The prophets said the Messiah must suffer these things before he begins his time of glory." Then he began to explain everything that had been written about himself in the Scriptures. He started with the books of Moses and then he talked about what the prophets had said about him.

They came near the town of Emmaus, and Jesus acted as if he did not plan to stop there. But they wanted him to stay. They begged him, "Stay with us. It's almost night. There's hardly any daylight left." So he went in to stay with them.

Joining them at the supper table, Jesus took some bread and gave thanks. Then he broke some off and gave it to them. Just then the men were allowed to recognize him. But when they saw who he was, he disappeared. They said to each other, "When he talked to us on the road, it felt like a fire burning in us. How exciting it was when he explained to us the true meaning of the Scriptures!"

So the two men got up then and went back to Jerusalem. There they found the followers of Jesus meeting together. The eleven apostles and the people with them said, "The Lord really has risen from death! He appeared to Simon."

Then the two men told what had happened on the road. They talked about how they recognized Jesus when he shared the bread with them.[380]

6.6 Jesus Appears to His Followers

The day was Sunday, and that same evening the followers were together. They had the doors locked because they were afraid of the Jewish leaders.[381]

While the two men were saying these things to the other followers, Jesus himself came and stood among them. He said to them, "Peace be with you."

This surprised the followers. They were afraid. They thought they were seeing a ghost.[382]

He criticized them because they had so little faith. They were stubborn and refused to believe the people who said Jesus had risen from death.[383]

But Jesus said, "Why are you troubled? Why do you doubt what you see? Look at my hands and my feet. It's really me. Touch me. You can see that I have a living body; a ghost does not have a body like this."

After Jesus told them this, he showed them his hands and his feet. The followers were amazed and very, very happy to see that Jesus was alive. They still could not believe what they saw. He said to them, "Do you have any food here?" They gave him a piece of cooked fish. While the followers watched, he took the fish and ate it.[384]

When the followers saw the Lord, they were very happy.

Then Jesus said again, "Peace be with you. It was the Father who sent me, and I am now sending you in the same way." Then he breathed on them and said, "Receive the Holy Spirit. If you forgive the sins of anyone, their sins are forgiven. If there is anyone whose sins you don't forgive, their sins are not forgiven."[385]

6.7 Jesus Appears to Thomas

Thomas (called Didymus) was one of the twelve, but he was not with the other followers when Jesus came. They told him, "We saw the Lord." Thomas said, "That's hard to believe. I will have to see the nail holes in his hands, put my finger where the nails were, and put my hand into his side. Only then will I believe it."

A week later the followers were in the house again, and Thomas was with them. The doors were locked, but Jesus came and stood among them. He said, "Peace be with you!" Then he said to Thomas, "Put your finger here. Look at my hands. Put your hand here in my side. Stop doubting and believe."

Thomas said to Jesus, "My Lord and my God!"

Jesus said to him, "You believe because you see me. Great blessings belong to the people who believe without seeing me!"[386]

6.8 Jesus Appears to Seven Followers

Later, Jesus appeared again to his followers by Lake Galilee. This is how it happened: Some of the followers were together—Simon Peter, Thomas (called Didymus), Nathanael from Cana in Galilee, the two sons of Zebedee, and two other followers. Simon Peter said, "I am going out to fish."

The other followers said, "We will go with you." So all of them went out and got into the boat. They fished that night but caught nothing.

Early the next morning Jesus stood on the shore. But the followers did not know it was Jesus. Then he said to them, "Friends, have you caught any fish?"

They answered, "No."

He said, "Throw your net into the water on the right side of your boat. You will find some fish there." So they did this. They caught so many fish that they could not pull the net back into the boat.

The follower Jesus loved very much said to Peter, "That man is the Lord!" When Peter heard him say it was the Lord, he wrapped his coat around himself. (He had taken his clothes off to work.) Then he jumped into the water. The other followers went to shore in the boat. They pulled the net full of fish. They were not very far from shore, only about 100 yards. When they stepped out of the boat and onto the shore, they saw a fire of hot coals. There were fish on the fire and some bread there too. Then Jesus said, "Bring some of the fish that you caught."

Simon Peter got into the boat and pulled the net to the shore. It was full of big fish—153 of them! But even with that many fish, the net did not tear. Jesus said to them, "Come and eat." None of the followers would ask him, "Who are you?" They knew he was the Lord. Jesus walked over to get the bread and gave it to them. He also gave them the fish.

This was now the third time Jesus appeared to his followers after he was raised from death.[387]

6.9 Jesus Talks to Peter

When they finished eating, Jesus said to Simon Peter, "Simon, son of John, do you love me more than these other men love me?"

Peter answered, "Yes, Lord, you know that I love you."

Then Jesus said to him, "Take care of my lambs."

Again Jesus said to him, "Simon, son of John, do you love me?"

Peter answered, "Yes, Lord, you know that I love you."

Then Jesus said, "Take care of my sheep."

A third time Jesus said, "Simon, son of John, do you love me?"

Peter was sad because Jesus asked him three times, "Do you love me?" He said, "Lord, you know everything. You know that I love you!"

Jesus said to him, "Take care of my sheep. The truth is, when you were young, you tied your own belt and went where you wanted. But when you are old, you will put out your hands, and someone else will tie your belt. They will lead you where you don't want to go." (Jesus said this to show how Peter would die to give glory to God.) Then he said to Peter, "Follow me!"

Peter turned and saw the follower Jesus loved very much walking behind them. (This was the follower who had leaned against Jesus at the supper and said, "Lord, who is it that will hand you over?") When Peter saw him behind them, he asked Jesus, "Lord, what about him?"

Jesus answered, "Maybe I want him to live until I come. That should not matter to you. You follow me!"

So a story spread among the followers of Jesus. They were saying that this follower would not die. But Jesus did not say he would not die. He only said, "Maybe I want him to live until I come. That should not matter to you."[388]

6.10 Jesus Gives His Followers a Mission

The eleven followers went to Galilee, to the mountain where Jesus told them to go. On the mountain the followers saw Jesus. They worshiped him. But some of the followers did not believe that it was really Jesus. So he came to them and said, "All authority in heaven and on earth is given to me. So go and make followers of all people in the world. Baptize them in the name of the Father and the Son and the Holy Spirit. Teach them to obey everything that I have told you to do.[389]

"Whoever believes and is baptized will be saved. But those who do not believe will be judged guilty. And the people who believe will be able to do these things as proof: They will use my name to force demons out of people. They will speak in languages they never learned. If they pick up snakes or drink any poison, they will not be hurt. They will lay their hands on sick people, and they will get well.[390]

"You can be sure that I will be with you always. I will continue with you until the end of time."[391]

6.11 Jesus' Final Instructions

This was after his death, but he showed them that he was alive, proving it to them in many ways. The apostles saw Jesus many times during the 40 days after he was raised from death. He spoke to them about God's kingdom. One time when Jesus was eating with them,[392]

Jesus said to them, "Remember when I was with you before? I said that everything written about me must happen—everything written in the Law of Moses, the books of the prophets, and the Psalms."

Then Jesus helped the followers understand these Scriptures about him. Jesus said to them, "It is written that the Messiah would be killed and rise from death on the third day. You saw these things happen—you are witnesses. You must go and tell people that they must change and turn to God, which will bring them his forgiveness. You must start from Jerusalem and tell this message in my name to the people of all nations. Remember that I will send you the one my Father promised. Stay in the city until you are given that power from heaven."[393]

He told them not to leave Jerusalem. He said, "Wait here until you receive what the Father promised to send. Remember, I told you about it before. John baptized people with water, but in a few days you will be baptized with the Holy Spirit."

The apostles were all together. They asked Jesus, "Lord, is this the time for you to give the people of Israel their kingdom again?"

Jesus said to them, "The Father is the only one who has the authority to decide dates and times. They are not for you to know. But the Holy Spirit will come on you and give you power. You will be my witnesses. You will tell people everywhere about me—in Jerusalem, in the rest of Judea, in Samaria, and in every part of the world."[394]

6.12 Jesus Is Carried Up Into Heaven

Jesus led his followers out of Jerusalem almost to Bethany. He raised his hands and blessed his followers. While he was blessing them, he was separated from them and carried into heaven.[395]

While they were watching, he went into a cloud, and they could not see him. They were staring into the sky where he had gone.

Suddenly two men wearing white clothes were standing beside them. They said, "Men from Galilee, why are you standing here looking into the sky? You saw Jesus carried away from you into heaven. He will come back in the same way you saw him go."[396]

After the Lord Jesus said these things to his followers, he was carried up into heaven. There, Jesus sat at the right side of God.[397]

They worshiped him and went back to Jerusalem very happy.[398] The Mount of Olives is about a half mile from Jerusalem.[399]

They stayed at the Temple all the time, praising God.[400]

6.13 The Coming of the Holy Spirit

When the day of Pentecost came, they were all together in one place. Suddenly a noise came from heaven. It sounded like a strong wind blowing. This noise filled the whole house where they were sitting. They saw something that looked like flames of fire. The flames were separated and stood over each person there. They were all filled with the Holy Spirit, and they began to speak different languages. The Holy Spirit was giving them the power to do this.

There were some godly Jews in Jerusalem at this time. They were from every country in the world. A large crowd came together because they heard the noise. They were surprised because, as the apostles were speaking, everyone heard in their own language.

They were all amazed at this. They did not understand how the apostles could do this. They said, "Look! These men we hear speaking are all from Galilee. But we hear them in our own languages. How is this possible? We are from all these different places: Parthia, Media, Elam, Mesopotamia, Judea, Cappadocia, Pontus, Asia, Phrygia, Pamphylia, Egypt, the areas of Libya near the city of Cyrene, Rome, Crete, and Arabia. Some of us were born Jews, and others have changed their religion to worship God like Jews. We are from these different countries, but we can hear these men in our own languages! We can all understand the great things they are saying about God."[401]

6.14 The Conclusion

The followers went everywhere in the world telling people the Good News, and the Lord helped them. By giving them power to do miracles the Lord proved that their message was true.[402]

There are many other things that Jesus did. If every one of them were written down, I think the whole world would not be big enough for all the books that would be written.[403]

Jesus did many other miraculous signs that his followers saw, which are not written in this book. But these are written so that you can believe that Jesus is the Christ, the Son of God. Then, by believing, you can have life through his name.[404]

The Family History of Jesus Christ According to Matthew

This is the family history of Jesus Christ. He came from the family of David and from the family of Abraham.

Abraham was the father of Isaac. Isaac was the father of Jacob. Jacob was the father of Judah and his brothers. Judah was the father of Perez and Zerah. (Their mother was Tamar.) Perez was the father of Hezron. Hezron was the father of Ram. Ram was the father of Amminadab. Amminadab was the father of Nahshon. Nahshon was the father of Salmon. Salmon was the father of Boaz. (His mother was Rahab.) Boaz was the father of Obed. (His mother was Ruth.) Obed was the father of Jesse. Jesse was the father of King David. David was the father of Solomon. (His mother had been Uriah's wife.)

Solomon was the father of Rehoboam. Rehoboam was the father of Abijah. Abijah was the father of Asa. Asa was the father of Jehoshaphat. Jehoshaphat was the father of Jehoram. Jehoram was the father of Uzziah. Uzziah was the father of Jotham. Jotham was the father of Ahaz. Ahaz was the father of Hezekiah. Hezekiah was the father of Manasseh. Manasseh was the father of Amon. Amon was the father of Josiah. Josiah was the grandfather of Jehoiachin and his brothers, who lived during the time that the people were taken away to Babylon.

After they were taken to Babylon: Jehoiachin was the father of Shealtiel. Shealtiel was the grandfather of Zerubbabel. Zerubbabel was the father of Abiud. Abiud was the father of Eliakim. Eliakim was the father of Azor. Azor was the father of Zadok. Zadok was the father of Achim. Achim was the father of Eliud. Eliud was the father of Eleazar. Eleazar was the father of Matthan. Matthan was the father of Jacob. Jacob was the father of Joseph. Joseph was the husband of Mary, and Mary was the mother of Jesus, who is called the Christ.

So there were fourteen generations from Abraham to David. There were also fourteen generations from David until the people were taken away to Babylon. And there were fourteen more from the time the people were taken to Babylon until the Messiah was born.[405]

The Family History of Jesus Christ According to Luke

When Jesus began to teach, he was about 30 years old. People thought that Jesus was Joseph's son.

Joseph was the son of Eli. Eli was the son of Matthat. Matthat was the son of Levi. Levi was the son of Melchi. Melchi was the son of

Jannai. Jannai was the son of Joseph. Joseph was the son of Mattathias. Mattathias was the son of Amos. Amos was the son of Nahum. Nahum was the son of Esli. Esli was the son of Naggai. Naggai was the son of Maath. Maath was the son of Mattathias. Mattathias was the son of Semein. Semein was the son of Josech. Josech was the son of Joda.

Joda was the son of Joanan. Joanan was the son of Rhesa. Rhesa was the son of Zerubbabel. Zerubbabel was the son of Shealtiel. Shealtiel was the son of Neri. Neri was the son of Melchi. Melchi was the son of Addi. Addi was the son of Cosam. Cosam was the son of Elmadam. Elmadam was the son of Er. Er was the son of Joshua. Joshua was the son of Eliezer. Eliezer was the son of Jorim. Jorim was the son of Matthat. Matthat was the son of Levi.

Levi was the son of Simeon. Simeon was the son of Judah. Judah was the son of Joseph. Joseph was the son of Jonam. Jonam was the son of Eliakim. Eliakim was the son of Melea. Melea was the son of Menna. Menna was the son of Mattatha. Mattatha was the son of Nathan. Nathan was the son of David. David was the son of Jesse. Jesse was the son of Obed. Obed was the son of Boaz. Boaz was the son of Salmon. Salmon was the son of Nahshon. Nahshon was the son of Amminadab. Amminadab was the son of Admin. Admin was the son of Arni. Arni was the son of Hezron. Hezron was the son of Perez. Perez was the son of Judah. Judah was the son of Jacob. Jacob was the son of Isaac. Isaac was the son of Abraham. Abraham was the son of Terah. Terah was the son of Nahor. Nahor was the son of Serug. Serug was the son of Reu. Reu was the son of Peleg. Peleg was the son of Eber. Eber was the son of Shelah.

Shelah was the son of Cainan. Cainan was the son of Arphaxad. Arphaxad was the son of Shem. Shem was the son of Noah. Noah was the son of Lamech. Lamech was the son of Methuselah. Methuselah was the son of Enoch. Enoch was the son of Jared. Jared was the son of Mahalaleel. Mahalaleel was the son of Cainan. Cainan was the son of Enos. Enos was the son of Seth. Seth was the son of Adam. Adam was the son of God.[406]

Timeline of the Life of Jesus

The following chart gives an idea of when Jesus actually lived according to the corrected calendar now in general use, though not every scholar agrees on these exact dates.

Date	Event
6 or 5 B.C.	Birth of Jesus
4 B.C.	Death of King Herod the Great
14 A.D.	Beginning of the reign of Tiberius Caesar in Rome
26 A.D.	Beginning of the work of John the Baptizer Baptism of Jesus Beginning of the public work of Jesus
27 A.D.	First Passover during the public work of Jesus
28 A.D.	Second Passover during the public work of Jesus
29 A.D.	Third Passover during the public work of Jesus
30 A.D.	Crucifixion of Jesus (Nisan/April 14)

Index

This index will help you match the Scripture portions used in this book with their sources—the books of Matthew, Mark, Luke, John, and Acts. This will enable you to examine them more closely in their original settings. Before each Scripture reference is a small number, which refers to the number at the end of each Scripture portion in the book. Also, the numbered section headings in this Index are the same as the ones in the book.

1 Thirty Years of Preparation

1.1 *The Beginning*
[1] Mark 1:1–2a
[2] Luke 1:1–4
[3] John 1:1–18

1.2 *The Birth of John the Baptizer Foretold*
[4] Luke 1:5–25

1.3 *The Birth of Jesus Foretold*
[5] Luke 1:26–38

1.4 *Mary Visits Elizabeth*
[6] Luke 1:39–45

1.5 *Mary Praises God*
[7] Luke 1:46–56

1.6 *The Birth of John the Baptizer*
[8] Luke 1:57–66

1.7 *Zechariah Praises God*
[9] Luke 1:67–80

1.8 *The Birth of Jesus*
[10] Matthew 1:18–25a
[11] Luke 2:1–7

1.9 *Shepherds Hear About Jesus*
[12] Luke 2:8-21

1.10 *Jesus Is Presented in the Temple*
[13] Luke 2:22-38

1.11 *Wise Men Come to Visit Jesus*
[14] Matthew 2:1-12

1.12 *Jesus' Family Escapes to Egypt*
[15] Matthew 2:13-15

1.13 *The Killing of Baby Boys in Bethlehem*
[16] Matthew 2:16-18

1.14 *Jesus' Family Returns From Egypt*
[17] Matthew 2:19-23

1.15 *The Boy Jesus at the Temple*
[18] Luke 2:40-52

2 Jesus' Public Life

2.1 *John the Baptizer Prepares the Way for Jesus*
[19] Luke 3:1-6
[20] Matthew 3:4-10
[21] Luke 3:10-18

2.2 *The Baptism of Jesus*
[22] Matthew 3:13-17
[23] Luke 3:23a

2.3 *The Temptation of Jesus*
[24] Matthew 4:1-11

2.4 *John the Baptizer Tells About the Messiah*
[25] John 1:19-28

2.5 *Jesus, the Lamb of God*
[26] John 1:29-34

2.6 *John Introduces His Followers to Jesus*
[27] John 1:35-42

2.7 Jesus Calls Phillip and Nathanael
28 John 1:43–51

2.8 Jesus' First Miraculous Sign
29 John 2:1–12

2.9 Jesus at the Temple
30 John 2:13–25

2.10 Jesus and Nicodemus
31 John 3:1–21

2.11 Jesus and John the Baptizer
32 John 3:22–4:3

2.12 John the Baptizer Put in Prison
33 Luke 3:19–20
34 Matthew 4:12a
35 Luke 4:14a

2.13 Jesus Talks to a Samaritan Woman
36 John 4:4–26

2.14 Jesus' Followers Return
37 John 4:27–38

2.15 Many Samaritans Believe
38 John 4:39–42

2.16 Jesus Returns to Galilee
39 John 4:43–45

2.17 Jesus Heals an Official's Son
40 John 4:46–54

2.18 Jesus Rejected in His Hometown
41 Luke 4:16–30

2.19 Jesus Begins Telling People the Good News
42 Matthew 4:13–17a
43 Mark 1:14b–15
44 Luke 4:14b–15

3 The Year of Popularity

3.1 Jesus Chooses Some Followers
  [45] Matthew 4:18-22
  [46] Luke 5:1-11

3.2 Jesus Frees a Man From an Evil Spirit
  [47] Mark 1:21-28

3.3 Jesus Heals Many People
  [48] Mark 1:29-34

3.4 Jesus Prays Alone
  [49] Mark 1:35-38

3.5 Jesus Teaches and Heals the People
  [50] Matthew 4:23-25

3.6 Jesus Heals a Sick Man
  [51] Mark 1:40-45

3.7 Jesus Heals a Crippled Man
  [52] Mark 2:1-12

3.8 Levi Follows Jesus
  [53] Mark 2:13-17

3.9 Jesus Answers a Question About Fasting
  [54] Luke 5:33-39

3.10 Jesus Heals a Man at a Pool
  [55] John 5:1-18

3.11 The Son Gives Life
  [56] John 5:19-30

3.12 Jesus Gives Proofs of His Authority
  [57] John 5:31-47

3.13 Jesus Is Lord Over the Sabbath Day
  [58] Mark 2:23-26
  [59] Matthew 12:5-7
  [60] Mark 2:27-28
  [61] Matthew 12:9-14

3.14 A Large Crowd Follows Jesus
  ⁶² Mark 3:7-12
  ⁶³ Matthew 12:17-21
  ⁶⁴ Luke 6:17-19

3.15 Jesus Chooses Twelve Apostles
  ⁶⁵ Luke 6:12-13
  ⁶⁶ Mark 3:14b-19

The Sermon on the Mount (3.16-34)

3.16 The People Who Receive God's Blessings
  ⁶⁷ Matthew 5:1-12

3.17 Jesus Calls His Followers Salt and Light
  ⁶⁸ Matthew 5:13-16

3.18 Jesus and the Law of Moses
  ⁶⁹ Matthew 5:17-20

3.19 Jesus Teaches About Anger
  ⁷⁰ Matthew 5:21-26

3.20 Jesus Teaches About Adultery
  ⁷¹ Matthew 5:27-30

3.21 Jesus Teaches About Divorce
  ⁷² Matthew 5:31-32

3.22 Jesus Teaches About Making Promises
  ⁷³ Matthew 5:33-37

3.23 Jesus Teaches About Fighting Back
  ⁷⁴ Matthew 5:38-42

3.24 Jesus Teaches About Loving Your Enemies
  ⁷⁵ Matthew 5:43-48

3.25 Jesus Teaches About Giving
  ⁷⁶ Matthew 6:1-4

3.26 Jesus Teaches About Prayer
  ⁷⁷ Matthew 6:5-15

3.27 Jesus Teaches About Fasting
  [78] Matthew 6:16–18

3.28 Jesus Teaches About What Is Important
  [79] Matthew 6:19–24

3.29 Jesus Teaches About Worry
  [80] Matthew 6:25–34

3.30 Jesus Teaches About Judging Others
  [81] Matthew 7:1–6

3.31 Ask God for What You Need
  [82] Matthew 7:7–12

3.32 The Narrow Gate and the Wide Gate
  [83] Matthew 7:13–14

3.33 What People Do Shows What They Are
  [84] Matthew 7:15–23

3.34 Two Kinds of People
  [85] Matthew 7:24–8:1

3.35 Jesus Heals an Officer's Servant
  [86] Matthew 8:5–13

3.36 Jesus Brings a Woman's Son Back to Life
  [87] Luke 7:11–17

3.37 Jesus and John the Baptizer
  [88] Luke 7:18–35

3.38 Jesus Offers Rest to His People
  [89] Matthew 11:25–30

3.39 Jesus and a Sinful Woman
  [90] Luke 7:36–50

3.40 Jesus in Galilee
  [91] Luke 8:1–3

3.41 Jesus' Power Is From God
  [92] Matthew 12:22–37

3.42 *Some People Doubt Jesus' Authority*
 ⁹³ Matthew 12:38–45

3.43 *Jesus' Followers Are His True Family*
 ⁹⁴ Matthew 12:46–50
 ⁹⁵ Luke 11:27–28

3.44 *The Story About the Farmer Sowing Seed*
 ⁹⁶ Matthew 13:1–23

3.45 *Use the Understanding You Have*
 ⁹⁷ Mark 4:21–25

3.46 *Jesus Uses the Story About the Growing Seed*
 ⁹⁸ Mark 4:26–29

3.47 *The Story About the Wheat and Weeds*
 ⁹⁹ Matthew 13:24–30

3.48 *The Stories About the Mustard Seed and the Yeast*
 ¹⁰⁰ Matthew 13:31–33
 ¹⁰¹ Mark 4:33–34
 ¹⁰² Matthew 13:35

3.49 *Jesus Explains the Story About the Weeds*
 ¹⁰³ Matthew 13:36–43

3.50 *The Stories About the Treasure and the Pearl*
 ¹⁰⁴ Matthew 13:44–46

3.51 *The Story About the Fishing Net*
 ¹⁰⁵ Matthew 13:47–53

3.52 *Jesus Calms the Storm*
 ¹⁰⁶ Mark 4:35–41

3.53 *Jesus Frees a Man From Evil Spirits*
 ¹⁰⁷ Luke 8:26–27
 ¹⁰⁸ Mark 5:3b–20

3.54 *Jesus Gives Life to a Dead Girl and Heals a Sick Woman*
 ¹⁰⁹ Mark 5:21–43

3.55 Jesus Heals Two Blind Men
    [110] Matthew 9:27-34

3.56 Jesus Rejected in His Hometown
    [111] Mark 6:1-6a

4 The Year of Opposition

4.1 Pray for Workers
    [112] Matthew 9:35-38

4.2 Jesus Sends Out the Twelve Apostles
    [113] Matthew 10:1
    [114] Matthew 10:5-42
    [115] Luke 9:6a
    [116] Mark 6:12b-13
    [117] Matthew 11:1

4.3 How John the Baptizer Was Killed
    [118] Mark 6:14-16
    [119] Matthew 14:2d
    [120] Mark 6:17-29
    [121] Matthew 14:12b

4.4 Jesus Feeds More Than Five Thousand
    [122] Mark 6:30-37
    [123] John 6:7-15a
    [124] Mark 6:45
    [125] Matthew 14:23a

4.5 Jesus Walks on the Water
    [126] Matthew 14:23b-33

4.6 Jesus Heals Many Sick People
    [127] Mark 6:53-56

4.7 Jesus, the Bread of Life
    [128] John 6:22-59

4.8 Many Followers Leave Jesus
    [129] John 6:60-7:1

4.9　God's Law and Human Traditions
130 Mark 7:1–15

4.10　Jesus Helps a Canaanite Woman
131 Matthew 15:12–28

4.11　Jesus Heals a Deaf Man
132 Mark 7:31
133 Matthew 15:30
134 Mark 7:32–36
135 Matthew 15:31a
136 Mark 7:37b
137 Matthew 15:31b

4.12　Jesus Feeds More Than Four Thousand
138 Matthew 15:32–39

4.13　Some People Doubt Jesus' Authority
139 Matthew 16:1–4

4.14　Jesus' Followers Misunderstand Him
140 Matthew 16:5–12

4.15　Jesus Heals a Blind Man in Bethsaida
141 Mark 8:22–26

4.16　Peter Says Jesus Is the Messiah
142 Matthew 16:13–20

4.17　Jesus Says He Must Die
143 Matthew 16:21–26
144 Luke 9:26
145 Matthew 16:27b–28

4.18　Jesus Is Seen With Moses and Elijah
146 Matthew 17:1
147 Luke 9:28c–29a
148 Matthew 17:2
149 Luke 9:30–33
150 Matthew 17:5–13

4.19 Jesus Frees a Boy From an Evil Spirit
151 Matthew 17:14-17
152 Mark 9:20-29

4.20 Jesus Talks About His Death and Resurrection
153 Mark 9:30-32

4.21 Jesus Teaches About Paying Taxes
154 Matthew 17:24-27

4.22 Who Is the Greatest in God's Kingdom?
155 Matthew 18:1-5
156 Mark 9:38-41
157 Matthew 18:6-12

4.23 When Someone Hurts You
158 Matthew 18:15-20

4.24 A Story About Forgiveness
159 Matthew 18:21-35

4.25 Following Jesus
160 Luke 9:57-62

4.26 Jesus Goes to the Festival of Shelters
161 John 7:2-13

4.27 Jesus Teaches at the Festival
162 John 7:14-24

4.28 The People Wonder if Jesus Is the Messiah
163 John 7:25-44

4.29 Some Jewish Leaders Refuse to Believe
164 John 7:45-52

4.30 A Woman Caught in Adultery
165 John 7:53-8:11

4.31 Jesus Is the Light of the World
166 John 8:12-30

4.32 The Children of Abraham
167 John 8:31-41

4.33 The Children of the Devil
168 John 8:42–47

4.34 Jesus Talks About Himself and Abraham
169 John 8:48–59

4.35 Jesus Heals a Man Born Blind
170 John 9:1–12

4.36 Some Religious Leaders Have Questions
171 John 9:13–34

4.37 Spiritual Blindness
172 John 9:35–41

4.38 The Shepherd and His Sheep
173 John 10:1–21

4.39 Jesus Sends Out Seventy-two of His Followers
174 Luke 10:1–24

4.40 The Most Important Commandment, the Story About the Good Samaritan
175 Luke 10:25–37

4.41 Martha and Mary
176 Luke 10:38–42

4.42 Jesus Teaches About Prayer
177 Luke 11:1–13

4.43 Jesus Criticizes the Religious Leaders
178 Luke 11:37–54

4.44 Warning and Encouragement
179 Luke 12:1–12

4.45 The Story About a Rich Fool
180 Luke 12:13–21

4.46 Following Jesus May Bring You Trouble
181 Luke 12:49–53

4.47 Change Your Hearts
182 Luke 13:1–9

4.48 Jesus Heals a Woman on the Sabbath
[183] Luke 13:10-17

4.49 The Jewish Leaders Against Jesus
[184] John 10:22-42

4.50 The Narrow Door
[185] Luke 13:22-30

4.51 Jesus Will Die in Jerusalem
[186] Luke 13:31-35

4.52 Jesus at a Pharisee's Home
[187] Luke 14:1-14

4.53 The Story About People Invited to the Dinner
[188] Luke 14:15-24

4.54 Decide if You Can Follow Me
[189] Luke 14:25-35

4.55 The Story About the Lost Sheep
[190] Luke 15:1-7

4.56 The Story About the Lost Coin
[191] Luke 15:8-10

4.57 The Story About the Lost Son
[192] Luke 15:11-32

4.58 The Story About the Dishonest Manager
[193] Luke 16:1-15

4.59 The Rich Man and the Poor Man
[194] Luke 16:19-31

4.60 Forgiveness, Faith, and Duty
[195] Luke 17:1-10

4.61 The Death of Lazarus
[196] John 11:1-16

4.62 Jesus Comforts the Sisters of Lazarus
[197] John 11:17-37

4.63 *Jesus Raises Lazarus From Death*
   [198] John 11:38-44

4.64 *Religious Leaders Plan to Kill Jesus*
   [199] John 11:45-54

4.65 *Jesus Heals Ten Men with Leprosy*
   [200] Luke 17:11-19

4.66 *The Coming of God's Kingdom*
   [201] Luke 17:20-37

4.67 *The Story of the Widow Who Would Not Give Up*
   [202] Luke 18:1-8

4.68 *The Story About the Pharisee and the Tax Collector*
   [203] Luke 18:9-14

4.69 *Jesus Teaches About Divorce*
   [204] Matthew 19:3-8
   [205] Mark 10:10-12
   [206] Matthew 19:10-12

4.70 *Jesus Welcomes Children*
   [207] Mark 10:13-16

4.71 *A Rich Man Refuses to Follow Jesus*
   [208] Matthew 19:16-19
   [209] Mark 10:20-21a
   [210] Matthew 19:21b-30

4.72 *The Story About Workers in the Vineyard*
   [211] Matthew 20:1-16

4.73 *Jesus Talks Again About His Death and Resurrection*
   [212] Luke 18:31-34

4.74 *A Mother Asks a Special Favor*
   [213] Matthew 20:20-28

4.75 *Jesus Heals a Blind Man Named Bartimaeus*
   [214] Mark 10:46-52

4.76 Zacchaeus the Tax Collector
215 Luke 19:1-10

4.77 The Story About the Ten Servants
216 Luke 19:11-28

4.78 Mary Pours Perfume on Jesus at Bethany
217 John 11:55-12:2a
218 Matthew 26:6b
219 John 12:2b-6
220 Mark 14:6-9
221 John 12:9-11

5 The Week Jesus Dies

5.1 Jesus Enters Jerusalem
222 John 12:12
223 Luke 19:29-36a
224 Mark 11:8-10
225 Luke 19:37-44
226 Matthew 21:10-11
227 Matthew 21:14-17

5.2 Jesus Says a Fig Tree Will Die
228 Mark 11:12-14

5.3 Jesus Forces Merchants Out of the Temple
229 Mark 11:15-17
230 Luke 19:47-48

5.4 Jesus Talks About His Death Again
231 John 12:20-36a

5.5 Some Jews Refuse to Believe in Jesus
232 John 12:36b-50
233 Mark 11:19

5.6 The Fig Tree Is Dry and Dead
234 Mark 11:20-25

5.7 Religious Leaders Doubt Jesus' Authority
235 Mark 11:27–33

5.8 The Story About the Two Sons
236 Matthew 21:28–32

5.9 The Story About the Wicked Farmers
237 Matthew 21:33
238 Mark 12:2–8
239 Matthew 21:40–46

5.10 The Story About the Wedding Feast
240 Matthew 22:1–14

5.11 Is It Right to Pay Taxes to Caesar or Not?
241 Matthew 22:15–22

5.12 Marriage and the Seven Brothers
242 Matthew 21:23–33

5.13 The Most Important Command
243 Matthew 22:34–36
244 Mark 12:29–31
245 Matthew 22:40
246 Mark 12:32–34a

5.14 Is the Messiah David's Son or David's Lord?
247 Matthew 22:41–46

5.15 Jesus Criticizes the Religious Leaders
248 Matthew 23:1–39

5.16 A Poor Widow Gives All She Has
249 Mark 12:41–44

5.17 Jesus Warns About the Future
250 Mark 13:1–13
251 Matthew 24:11–31
252 Luke 21:28–33

5.18 Only God Knows When the Time Will Be
253 Matthew 24:36–41
254 Luke 21:34–36

[255] Mark 13:34-37
[256] Matthew 24:41-51

5.19 The Story About the Ten Girls
[257] Matthew 25:1-13

5.20 The Story About the Three Servants
[258] Matthew 25:14-30

5.21 The Son of Man Will Judge All People
[259] Matthew 25:31-46

5.22 The Plan to Kill Jesus
[260] Matthew 26:1-5

5.23 Judas Agrees to Help Jesus' Enemies
[261] Luke 22:3-4
[262] Matthew 26:15-16

5.24 Preparations for the Passover Meal
[263] Luke 22:7-13

Jesus' Last Supper with His Followers (5.25-40)

5.25 Who Is the Most Important?
[264] Luke 22:14a
[265] Luke 22:24-30

5.26 Jesus Washes His Followers' Feet
[266] John 13:3-17

5.27 Jesus Tells Who Will Turn Against Him
[267] John 13:18-20
[268] Luke 22:15-16
[269] Matthew 26:21
[270] John 13:22
[271] Matthew 26:22
[272] John 13:23-26a
[273] Matthew 26:24-25
[274] John 13:26b-30

5.28 The New Agreement From God
275 Luke 22:17-18
276 Matthew 26:26
277 Luke 22:19b-20a
278 Matthew 26:27b
279 Luke 22:20b
280 Matthew 26:28b-29

5.29 Jesus Gives a New Command
281 John 13:31-35

5.30 Jesus Says Peter Will Deny Him
282 John 13:36-37
283 Matthew 26:31-33
284 Luke 22:31-33
285 John 13:38a
286 Mark 14:30b-31
287 Luke 22:35-38

5.31 Jesus Comforts His Followers
288 John 14:1-4

5.32 Jesus Is the Only Way to the Father
289 John 14:5-14

5.33 Jesus Promises the Holy Spirit
290 John 14:15-31

5.34 Jesus Is Like a Vine
291 John 15:1-17

5.35 Jesus Warns His Followers
292 John 15:18-16:4b

5.36 The Work of the Holy Spirit
293 John 16:4c-15

5.37 Sadness Will Turn Into Happiness
294 John 16:16-33

5.38 Jesus Talks to His Father
295 John 17:1-5

5.39 Jesus Prays for His Followers
²⁹⁶ John 17:6-19

5.40 Jesus Prays for All Who Will Believe in Him
²⁹⁷ John 17:20-26

5.41 Jesus Prays Alone
²⁹⁸ Matthew 26:30
²⁹⁹ Matthew 26:36-39
³⁰⁰ Luke 22:43-44
³⁰¹ Matthew 26:40-46

5.42 Jesus Is Arrested
³⁰² John 18:2-9
³⁰³ Matthew 26:48-49
³⁰⁴ Luke 22:48
³⁰⁵ Mark 14:46
³⁰⁶ John 18:10
³⁰⁷ Luke 22:51
³⁰⁸ John 18:11a
³⁰⁹ Matthew 26:52b
³¹⁰ John 18:11b
³¹¹ Matthew 26:53-56
³¹² Mark 14:51-52

5.43 Jesus Is Brought Before Annas
³¹³ John 18:12-14
³¹⁴ John 18:24
³¹⁵ Matthew 26:57

5.44 Peter's First Denial of Jesus
³¹⁶ John 18:15-16
³¹⁷ John 18:18
³¹⁸ Mark 14:66
³¹⁹ John 18:17a
³²⁰ Mark 14:67b-68

5.45 The High Priest Questions Jesus
³²¹ John 18:19-23

5.46 Peter's Second and Third Denial
[322] John 18:25a
[323] Mark 14:69–70
[324] John 18:26
[325] Mark 14:71
[326] Luke 22:60b–62

5.47 Jesus Before the High Council
[327] Mark 14:55–56
[328] Matthew 26:60b–61
[329] Mark 14:58–65
[330] Luke 22:66–71

5.48 Judas Kills Himself
[331] Matthew 27:1–10

5.49 Jesus Is Brought Before Pilate
[332] John 18:28–38
[333] Luke 23:2
[334] Mark 15:4–5
[335] Luke 23:5–7

5.50 Pilate Sends Jesus to King Herod
[336] Luke 23:8–12

5.51 Pilate Tries to Free Jesus
[337] Mark 15:6–8
[338] Luke 23:13–15
[339] Matthew 27:17–21

5.52 Jesus Is Handed Over to Be Crucified
[340] John 19:1–15
[341] Matthew 27:24–25
[342] Luke 23:24–25

5.53 Pilate's Soldiers Make Fun of Jesus
[343] Matthew 27:27–31

5.54 Jesus Is Nailed to a Cross
[344] Luke 23:26–32
[345] Matthew 27:33–34
[346] Luke 23:33–34a

    347 John 19:23-24
    348 John 19:19-22
    349 Matthew 27:39-43
    350 Luke 23:39-43
    351 John 19:25-27

5.55 Jesus Dies
    352 Matthew 27:45-47
    353 John 19:28-30a
    354 Luke 23:46
    355 Matthew 27:51-54
    356 John 19:31-37

5.56 Jesus Is Buried
    357 John 19:38-40
    358 Matthew 27:60
    359 Mark 15:47
    360 Luke 23:56

5.57 The Tomb of Jesus Is Guarded
    361 Matthew 27:62-66

6 The Last Forty Days

6.1 The Resurrection of Jesus
    362 Mark 16:1a
    363 Matthew 28:2-4
    364 Mark 16:1bc-4
    365 Luke 24:3-5ab
    366 Mark 16:6ab
    367 Luke 24:5c
    368 Mark 16:6cd
    369 Luke 24:6-7
    370 Mark 16:7
    371 Luke 24:8
    372 Matthew 28:8
    373 Luke 24:10-12a
    374 John 20:3-10

6.2 Jesus Appears to Mary Magdalene
375 Mark 16:9
376 John 20:11-18
377 Mark 16:11

6.3 Jesus Appears to Others
378 Matthew 28:9-10

6.4 The Guards Report to the Religious Leaders
379 Matthew 28:11-15

6.5 On the Road to Emmaus
380 Luke 24:13-35

6.6 Jesus Appears to His Followers
381 John 20:19
382 Luke 24:36-37
383 Mark 16:14b
384 Luke 24:38-43
385 John 20:20b-23

6.7 Jesus Appears to Thomas
386 John 20:24-29

6.8 Jesus Appears to Seven Followers
387 John 21:1-14

6.9 Jesus Talks to Peter
388 John 21:15-23

6.10 Jesus Gives His Followers a Mission
389 Matthew 28:16-20a
390 Mark 16:16-18
391 Matthew 28:20b

6.11 Jesus' Final Instructions
392 Acts 1:3-4a
393 Luke 24:44-49
394 Acts 1:4b-8

6.12 Jesus Is Carried Up Into Heaven
395 Luke 24:50-51
396 Acts 1:9b-11

[397] Mark 16:19
[398] Luke 24:52
[399] Acts 1:12b
[400] Luke 24:53

6.13 The Coming of the Holy Spirit
[401] Acts 2:1–11

6.14 The Conclusion
[402] Mark 16:20
[403] John 21:25
[404] John 20:30–31

The Family History of Jesus Christ According to Matthew
[405] Matthew 1:1–17

The Family History of Jesus Christ According to Luke
[406] Luke 3:23–38